JOHN KEATS
Against All Doubtings

Andrew Keanie

GREENWICH EXCHANGE
LONDON

Greenwich Exchange, London

JOHN KEATS
Against All Doubtings
©Andrew Keanie 2013

First published in Great Britain in 2013
All rights reserved

Printed and bound by **imprint**digital.net
Typesetting and layout by Jude Keen Limited, London
Tel: 020 8355 4541
Cover design by December Publications, Belfast
Tel: 028 90286559
Cover image ©Mary Evans Picture Library

Greenwich Exchange Website: www.greenex.co.uk

Cataloguing in Publication Data is available
from the British Library.

ISBN: 978-1-906075-75-0

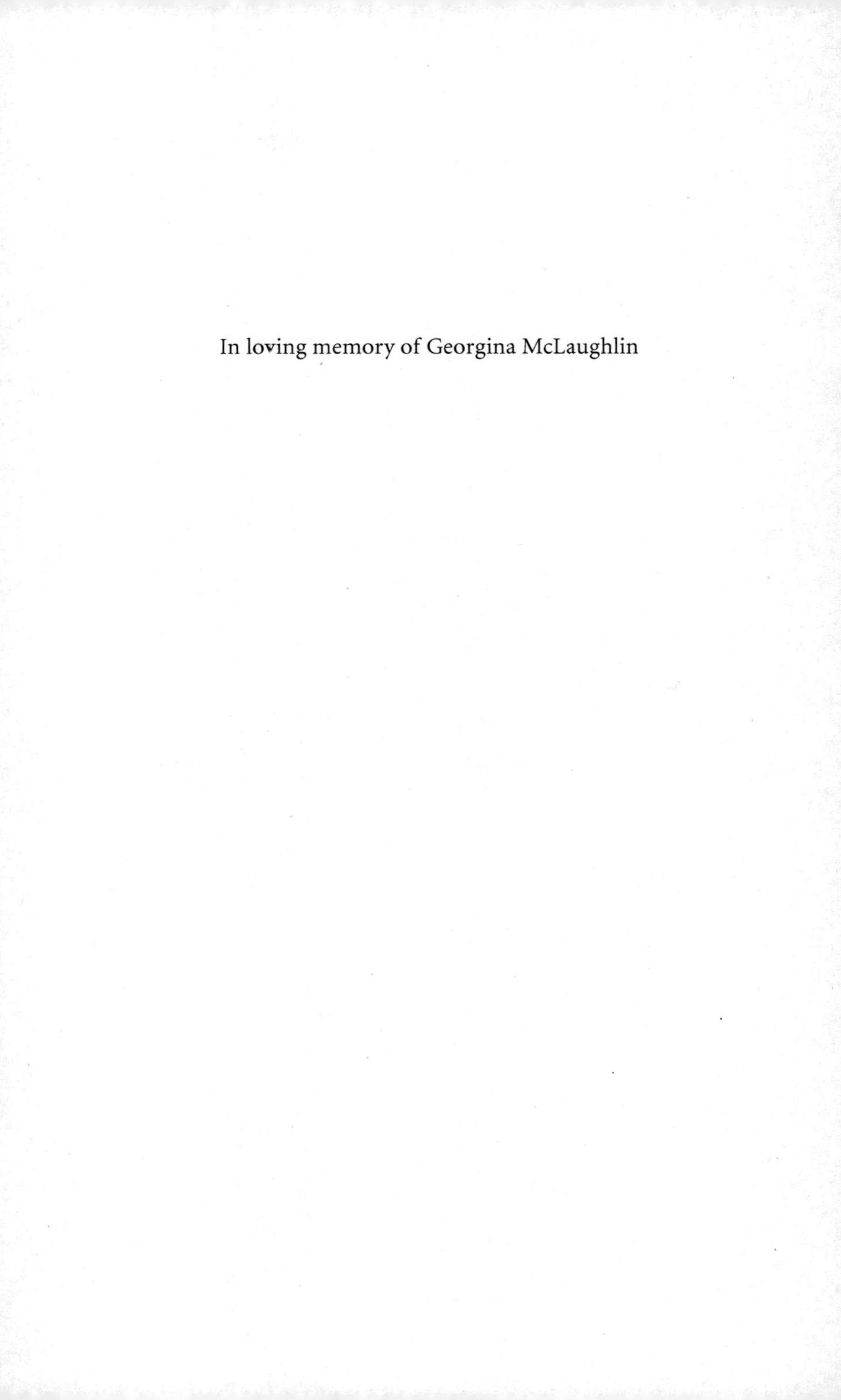

In loving memory of Georgina McLaughlin

In memory of Professor Robert Welch

Contents

Introduction

The magazines that reviewed Keats's work were keen to uphold what they saw as the tenets of Augustan poetry – John Dryden (1631-1700), Alexander Pope (1688-1744) and Dr Samuel Johnson (1709-84). It was a losing battle since the manners and fashions of the time were changing. Many of the magazine-reviewers and their readers resisted William Wordsworth (1770-1850) and Samuel Taylor Coleridge (1772-1834). Charles James Fox (1749-1806), a lover of classical literature, said to Coleridge, 'I am not of your party, Sir', which says a lot. It states a position that is aristocratic and privileged. Wordsworth, Coleridge, and later Keats, were neither. Privilege also meant a classical education. A literary man was expected to have been classically educated.

Though you are reading this book about one of the greatest young dreamers and poets who ever lived, you will probably have been influenced first by the current scientism that is so unpropitious to dreams and thus hostile to real poets. In this ethos, dreams are the individual's and are un-recordable by technology, and are therefore of doubtful material status. Poetry full of imagery and feeling has few outlets unlike, say, the poetry – chopped up prose sentences – that gets published in the *TLS* and elsewhere.

Having trained as a doctor in Guy's Hospital, London, Keats knew about material existence in more than enough empirical ways (including anatomy, botany, chemistry and physiology) to be counted a 'man of the world'. He knew about suffering. He could explain, for example, the difference between a sore throat and syphilis. (Gittings, p.343) He would have had to deal emotionally with the noises made, for example, by a child patient having a limb amputated without anaesthetic. He nursed his consumptive brother Tom (1799-1818) to the bitter end; and he felt the sweetness of his feelings for the love of his life, Fanny Brawne (1800-65), turn to bitterness and tears even as his own tuberculosis drove him to Italy in search of better health, and finally to his Roman deathbed in 1821.

He also knew about the distinction, and the relationship, between dreams that perplex and poetry that heals:

> Art thou not of the dreamer tribe?
> The poet and the dreamer are distinct,
> Diverse, sheer opposite, antipodes.
> The one pours out a balm upon the World,
> The other vexes it. (*The Fall of Hyperion: A Dream*, I, 198-202)

If the public understanding of Keats's work was flattened during his short lifetime into reviews fit for a conformist readership, those very reviews can (and in this study will) be evoked to garland his achievement as all the more gorgeous and irreducible. Some of the most eloquent contemporary attacks on geniuses often come to seem like encomia. (For about 150 years after his death in 1616, Shakespeare's achievement was considered disputable because of his works' lack of classical form.) However, it has to be added that downright neglect of Keats's work would hold back the rise of his reputation at least as much as did the aggression against him during his lifetime. For nearly two decades after his death, not one reprint of his poems was published in England. In 1835, Keats's publisher, John Taylor (1781-1864), had serious doubts about venturing to publish the poet's work again: ' ... but the world cares nothing for him – I fear that even 250 copies would not sell'. On this basis most poetry published in Britain today would not be published at all. A copy of his *Poems* (1817) that Keats had given to Wordsworth was found after Wordsworth's death over three decades later with its pages still uncut. The first biographical study of the poet – Richard Monckton Milnes's (1809-1885) *Life, Letters, and Literary Remains of John Keats* – was not published until 1848. It would take until a century after Keats's birth for him to be established as a canonical writer. In the meantime, the fact that his poetry was often a point of contention for the Victorians – such as Matthew Arnold (1822-88), Gerard Manley Hopkins (1844-89) and Walter Pater (1839-94) – indicates fame.

1

Humble Origins, Politics and Poetry

He lost his father (who had been the head ostler at the Swan and Hoop, Finsbury, London) at the age of nine. He lost his mother at fourteen. Orphaned, and with no guardian in the world but the solicitor, Richard Abbey, he had to look after his younger brothers, George and Tom, and his younger sister, Fanny. His life was not easy. George's decision to emigrate to America in June 1818 affected him deeply. So did Tom's death later that same year. So too did his separation from Fanny, who had to stay with the Abbey family in Walthamstow. Keats and his sister clearly felt aggrieved by Abbey's cold attitude towards them, which involved restricting Fanny's freedom, giving them little money, and keeping them apart. (*Letters*, I, pp.62-3) Abbey actually denied Fanny Keats the opportunity to visit Tom in the final stages of his illness in November 1818. Keats could rarely get out of bed in the morning feeling happy and thinking 'this day is my own'. He could not listen to the nightingale on Hampstead Heath, nor visualise the Grecian urn, so much with a weekday poet's leisurely solicitude as with a longing for it. 'This is the world', he told George in March 1819, 'thus we cannot expect to give away many hours to pleasure – Circumstances are like Clouds continually gathering and bursting – While we are laughing the seed of some trouble is put into the wide arable land of events – while we are laughing it sprouts ... grows and suddenly bears a poison fruit which we must pluck.' (*Letters*, II, p.79) He never made any money from writing.

He did visit Scotland, the north of Ireland and the Lake District, and found on his travels sublime scenery and savage poverty, but more typically he visited the sort of down-at-heel locations that were so un-poetically populated by budget holidaymakers during peak seasons: say, Margate, or Shanklin (on the Isle of Wight), or Burford Bridge (Surrey); not Coleridge's Quantocks nor his Hartz Mountains, not Wordsworth's Alps, and not Lord Byron's (1788-1824) glittering and heaving Mediterranean, nor Percy Bysshe Shelley's (1792-1822) storm-lashed woods outside Florence. Having lived in Britain all his short life, Keats's chief purpose in going to Italy was vainly to prolong his life, actually to die.

He lived and worked in a land already considered claustrophobic by poets with visionary intelligence and liberal inclinations – a land of hedges and sheep, a land of Anglicanism and collectors and curators of culture (usually excluding anything to do with, say, Catholic Dante's Paolo and Francesca), a land of lowered horizons. 'I sometimes feel a languishment,' he wrote in 'Happy is England! I could be content' (1816), 'For skies Italian, and an inward groan/To sit upon an Alp as on a throne'. England's self-image was one of orderliness and scrupulousness, yet underneath this there was a collective, inchoate anger that could suddenly erupt in the sort of purple-faced, finger-thrusting, spit-marked philistinism that disturbed the preferred appearance of learned equanimity. For example, on 5 August 1822, the London *Courier* pronounced that 'Shelley, the writer of some infidel poetry, has been drowned; *now* he knows whether there is a God or no.' Such a land was perceived and presided over by conservative critics, whose readers included (of course) members of conservative clubs whose favourite books were sedatives. Keats could not have been sincere and got on in such a world. He could not have declared himself a poet, endeavouring to celebrate or stimulate imaginative beauty, and realistically have expected to escape with a whole skin.

His first big poetic romance, *Endymion* (1817-18), was manhandled and mauled at the time by reviewers because of his 'low' birth, his second-rate education (we would say vocational education – Shakespeare catches the mood in his reference to 'rude mechanics'), his political radicalism, and the 'lax morality' presumed to be a result of these hereditary shortcomings. From 1815, he was a friend of, and admired by, the controversial editor of the weekly *Examiner*, Leigh Hunt (1784-1859): 'Mr Keats is no half-painter, who has only distinct ideas occasionally, and fills up the rest with commonplaces. He feels all as he goes. In his best pieces, every bit is precious; and he knew it, and laid it on as carefully as Titian or Giorgione ... There are stanzas, for which Persian kings would fill a poet's mouth with gold' (*Leigh Hunt: Selected Writings*, pp.107-8). Hunt had served time in Surrey Gaol (1813-14), and he had had to pay a fine of £500 (and give a security of £750 for good conduct during five years) for libelling the Prince Regent. In March 1812, Hunt's offence had been to hit out simultaneously at the monarchy and the sycophantic mainstream press by complaining that English newspaper readers would never know that such a '*delightful, blissful, wise, pleasurable, honourable, virtuous, true and immortal* PRINCE, was a violator of his word, a libertine over head and ears in debt and disgrace, a despiser of domestic ties, the companion of gamblers and demireps, a man who has just closed half a century without one single claim on the gratitude of his country or the respect of posterity!' (*Examiner*, March 1812) A friend of Hunt's was not a friend of the Establishment. Hunt's paternal lineage could be traced to West India, and his dark hair, dark skin and thick lips made a wonderful target of him for British journalists whose duty it was to fend off foreign influence.

Keats was eager to meet this arch-fiend of contemporary counter-culture. His friend, Charles Cowden Clarke (1787-1877), had already spent time in Hunt's electrifying company, and when Clarke told Keats about the experiences, the poet's keenness to meet Hunt was sharpened even more. Keats produced the following lines, 'Written On the Day That Mr. Leigh Hunt Left Prison', in February 1815:

> What though for showing truth to flatter'd state,
> Kind Hunt was shut in prison, yet has he,
> In his immortal spirit, been as free
> As the sky-searching lark, and as elate.

During his time in prison, Hunt enjoyed the support of his family and his many liberal-minded friends. His visitors included (the by-now famous) Byron (charmed by 'the wit in the dungeon') and Shelley. Shelley was 'boiling with indignation at the horrible injustice & tyranny of the sentence pronounced on Hunt', and his solidarity with Hunt was unequivocal. 'Surely,' Shelley told his friend, the bookseller Thomas Hookham (1786-1867), 'the seal of abjectness & slavery is indelibly stamped upon the character of England.' (15 February 1813) But Byron and Shelley were not in Keats's modest, and therefore vulnerable, position in society. They were aristocrats unattached to the strings of petty-bourgeois embarrassment that can be twitched with such hateful knowingness by hacks (so often hired to provide people with so much to look down upon that they forget to look up). Keats told Benjamin Bailey (1791-1853) in 1817 that he was 'disgusted with literary Men', and two years later he told his brother: 'You see what it is to be under six foot and not a lord.'

Keats's impetuous and youthful support for Hunt was in some sense a forward-payment for Hunt's admiration of his poetic gift. There is the sense that Keats's lines (quoted above, and below) make up in effect his application for inclusion in Hunt's literary coterie, which at the time included the historical painter and art critic, Benjamin Haydon (1786-1846), the essayist, Charles Lamb (1775-1834) and the Irish poet, Thomas Moore (1779-1852). It is possible that at this point Keats, like many young people, was high-minded and energised with enthusiasms he did not quite mean, and it may have been the case that he guessed going public with an initial commitment to Hunt's politics would help him on his way towards the truest 'Temple of Fame' (*Letters*, I, p.170):

> Minion of grandeur! think you [Hunt] did wait?
>   Think you he naught but prison walls did see,
>   Till, so unwilling, thou unturn'dst the key?
> Ah, no! far happier, nobler was his fate!
> In Spenser's halls he stray'd, and bowers fair,
>   Culling enchanted flowers; and he flew
> With daring Milton through the fields of air:
>   To regions of his own his genius true
> Took happy flights. Who shall his fame impair
>   When thou art dead, and all thy wretched crew?

Not yet having alchemised his own 'jumbled heap' of thoughts and feelings into 'images of thoughts refin'd' ('O Solitude! if I must with thee dwell'), Keats was admiring, and aspiring to, the dignity of inner riches that made Hunt superior to his persecutors, and self-contained despite his imprisonment. 'The busy time is just gone by,' said Keats to Clarke on leaving the medical profession to become a poet, 'and I can now devote any time you may mention to the pleasure of seeing Mr Hunt – 'twill be an Era in my existence.'

The term used for many of those associated with Hunt, including the republican essayist, William Hazlitt (1778-1830), was 'Cockney'. In an influential article, the redoubtable 'Z' said that Hunt

> is the ideal of a Cockney Poet. He raves perpetually about 'green fields', 'jaunty streams', and 'o'er-arching leafiness', exactly as a Cheapside shop-keeper does about the beauties of his box on the Camberwell road. Mr Hunt is altogether unacquainted with the face of nature in her magnificent scenes; he has never seen any mountain higher than Highgate-hill, nor reclined by any stream more pastoral than the Serpentine River. But he is determined to be a poet eminently rural, and he rings the changes – till one is sick of him, on the beauties of the different 'high views' which

he has taken of God and nature, in the course of some Sunday
dinner parties, at which he has assisted in the neighbourhood of
London. ('Cockney School I', *Blackwood's Edinburgh Magazine*)

'Cockney' quickly became part of the condescending parlance of established cultural commentators for whom any sympathiser with Hunt was either a typically minor irritant to be routinely eradicated or a full-scale menace to be fought with heavier rhetorical artillery – it could depend on the offender's estimated capacity to damage the British reactionary spirit, or as it might be put, to displace the Establishment. Keats's (perhaps rather naive, or shrewd, or a bit of both) advocacy of Hunt was treated more as a minor irritant. Later, Keats's greatest poetry would merely be considered ripe for a sort of nastily playful lampooning.

Shelley claimed that Keats's death was hastened by his treatment at the hands of vindictive reviewers, writing to Charles Ollier (1788-1859), his publisher, about his new 'poem entitled "Adonais". It is a lament on the death of poor Keats, with some interposed stabs on the assassins of his peace and of his fame.' (*Shelley Letters*, II, p.297) If Shelley's sense of solidarity with the imprisoned Hunt had been heartfelt, his empathy with the calumniated Keats was – and remains – vascular with admiration:

> He has outsoared the shadow of our night;
> Envy and calumny and hate and pain,
> And that unrest which men miscall delight,
> Can touch him not and torture not again;
> From the contagion of the world's slow stain
> He is secure … (XL)

> He is a portion of that loveliness
> Which once he made more lovely; he doth bear
> His part, while the one Spirit's plastic stress
> Sweeps through the dull dense world … (XLIII).

Despite the magnificence of his poetic tribute to Keats, Shelley's Preface to *Adonais* does, unfortunately, seem to reduce both Shelley's and Keats's visionary *raisons d'être* to a daftly defiant entrenchment in a dream of how things work in the world – a pair of ineffectual angels, perhaps. The following, for example, can serve to illustrate how Shelley exposed both himself and his subject to further ridicule: 'The savage criticism of *Endymion*, which appeared in the *Quarterly Review*, produced the most violent effect on [Keats's] susceptible mind; the agitation thus originated ended in the rupture of a blood-vessel in the lungs; a rapid consumption ensued, and the succeeding acknowledgements from more candid critics of the true greatness of his powers were ineffectual to heal the wound thus wantonly afflicted.' (Preface, *Adonais*, 1821) This is the kind of talk that one reads in the novels of Shelley's friend, the satirist, Thomas Love Peacock (1785-1866). In *Headlong Hall* (1816) and *Nightmare Abbey* (1818), Peacock made affectionate fun of many of the preposterous conceits of the Romantic writers of the day (though the author of the Preface to *Adonais* appears to have resisted the Peacock corrective and retained at least some Romantic preposterousness). Byron, however, did not upholster every satirical blow he delivered with affection. Byron had little time for the poetry of a former apothecary with pretensions, and he had almost as little time for talk of medical matters coming from his notably unworldly friend, Shelley. In a typical instance of exultant profanity in *Don Juan*, Byron would allude to the subject of 'John Keats, who was killed off by one critique'. In saying this, Byron was poking private fun at Shelley's indulgent précis of Keats's 'martyrdom' as much as public fun at Keats: 'Poor fellow! His was an untoward fate;/'Tis strange the mind, that very fiery particle,/Should let itself be snuffed out by an article.' (*Don Juan*, XI, lx) Given Shelley's ostracisation, and given Byron's instinctive knowledge of how to market himself (the latter noted his own response to a bad review was to consume three bottles of claret), it would be a very long time before Keats's drolly smothered spark would mount into universally recognised starry brightness.

As already mentioned, the politics of Hunt and his 'Cockney' circle were often acidly expressed, and this elicited strong feelings in readers. Broadly speaking, the Cockneys' attitude was a continuation of the English Jacobinism of the 1790s (when even the most discreet nods of sympathy towards Revolutionary France would be exposed and excoriated in, for example, the pages of the *Edinburgh Review*). Many of Keats's earliest poems contain bluntly republican points of view. 'On Peace' is a call to the crowned heads of Europe to use their power and success for universal freedom:

> O Europe! let not sceptered tyrants see
> That thou must shelter in thy former state;
> Keep thy chains burst, and boldly say thou art free;
> Give thy kings law – leave not uncurbed the great
> So with the horrors past thou'lt win thy happier fate!

The poems to Thaddeus Kosciusko (1746-1817), the general who led an unsuccessful revolt against the partitioning of his native Poland (1794), express the view that Kosciusko is part of a perennial political integrity traceable back to King Alfred (849-99), the founder of the Saxon Constitution of England:

> When some good spirit walks upon the earth,
>   Thy name with Alfred's, and the great of yore
> Gently commingling, gives tremendous birth
> To a loud hymn, that sounds far, far away … ('To Kosciusko').

The title page of Keats's first published collection, *Poems* (1817), had a dedication to Hunt, and there was also a picture of Shakespeare and a few lines quoted from Edmund Spenser (1552-99). This all combined to present a passionate assertion of Keats's political sympathies. Hunt's leading articles for *The Examiner* regularly invoked writers like Chaucer (1340-1400), Shakespeare and Spenser as the custodians of English freedom, and now Keats's *Poems* was almost certainly going to irritate conservatives in that it was published on 3 March 1817 (a Monday), which immediately followed Hunt's keen censure (in the Sunday's *Examiner*) of the Foreign Secretary Lord Castlereagh's (1769-1822) part in trying to suspend the habeas corpus act. Hunt's article, 'On the Proposed Suspension of the Habeas Corpus Act', called Castlereagh 'a man, who is proved guilty in the House of Commons of violating the Constitution and setting at nought the representative rights of the people, coming forward and asking for a suspension of our most sacred privilege'. Furthermore, Hunt warned readers that 'The Suspension Bill, if it pass, will be an unconstitutional assumption of power by the House of Commons illegally constituted.' Given the timing, the publication of Keats's new *Poems* was tantamount to an announcement of the poet's concurrence with the author of the leader in *The Examiner*.

The first stanza of the poem, 'Written on 29 May, the Anniversary of the Restoration of Charles the 2nd', is addressed abrasively to politically sleepwalking British citizens, and the second stanza invokes again the individuals already championed by Hunt:

Infatuate Britons, will you still proclaim
His memory, your direst, foulest shame?
    Nor patriots revere?

Ah! while I hear each traitorous lying bell,
'Tis gallant Sydney's, Russel's, Vane's sad knell,
    That pains my wounded ear.

The man mentioned in the second stanza, Algernon Sydney (1622-83), the author of *Discourses Concerning Government*, was the English Whig politician beheaded for his supposed part in the Rye House Plot to assassinate Charles II. Keats had learned from reading Gilbert Burnet's (1643-1715) *History of My Own Times* (2 volumes, 1724 and 1734) that Sydney was 'a republican of most extraordinary courage'. But now (according to Keats), in the nineteenth century, crowds of 'Infatuate Britons' were uncritically enjoying the festivities organised by a corrupt Prince Regent.

How strongly did Keats really feel about the immorality of his fellow-citizens' celebrations? Andrew Motion says that 'Unlike several of his friends, notably Hazlitt, Keats did not allow his disappointment with domestic politics to convert into hero-worship of Napoleon.' (Motion, 584) Were Keats's republican leopard-spots paint or did they go all the way through? The earlier poems, such as 'Written on 29 May', are his most overtly political ones. They are accomplished and stirringly subversive, but they are not what the poet is best remembered for. They were scarcely given any attention at the time. Clarke said that *Poems* 'might have emerged in Timbuktoo with far stronger chance of fame and approbation … The whole community, as if by compact, seemed determined to know nothing about it.' In June 1817, there was an anonymous review in the *Anti-Gallican Monitor*: 'this dress is made by a great-grandchild of Milton, after the poet's mode; but the white crepe in his buttonhole, a token of grief for the loss of his liberty, is on the ground of Milton's political principles – Poor youth!' James Ollier, the publisher of *Poems*, would express in forthright terms his reasons for dropping the collection:

> By far the greater number of persons who have purchased it from
> us have found fault with it in such plain terms, that we have in
> many cases offered to take the book back rather than be annoyed
> with the ridicule which has, time after time, been showered upon
> it. In fact, it was only on Saturday last that we were under the
> mortification of having our own opinion of its merits flatly

contradicted by a gentleman, who told us he considered it 'no better than a take in'. These are unpleasant imputations for any one in business to labour under …

Hunt felt that these early offerings from Keats – 'the impatient workings of the younger god within him' (*Indicator*, August 1820) – were the forerunners of the best kind of royalty.

2

'On First Looking into Chapman's Homer'

Keats's sonnet, 'On First Looking into Chapman's Homer' (1816), shows two things about the poet: his lack of classical education and the reality of his burgeoning genius. It is also an Epiphany – a conversion of a man into a poet with a vision. Mundanely, he was not able to read the Greek poet Homer until his discovery of an English translation by the Elizabethan poet, George Chapman (1559-1634). Once introduced to the magnificence of ancient Greek poetry (albeit at a remove), Keats would retain and renew an extraordinary raptness with this world for the rest of his life:

> Much have I travell'd in the realms of gold,
>> And many goodly states and kingdoms seen;
>> Round many western islands have I been
> Which bards in fealty to Apollo hold.
> Oft of one wide expanse had I been told
>> That deep-brow'd Homer ruled as his demesne;
>> Yet did I never breathe its pure serene
> Till I heard Chapman speak out loud and bold …

Having in previous poems rather formally esteemed Hunt's ability to 'travel' in dreams and poetry, now Keats had begun to do some extravagant, inspirational, and unguarded travelling of his own. He had just discovered in himself a heroic amplitude in a different dimension – the 'mental space' that Coleridge had appreciated in the poetry of Spenser. The sense of wonder is infectious: 'Then felt I like some watcher of the skies/When a new planet swims into his ken … '. There is the joyousness of discovery in these two lines. The age of science and wonder in which he lived is undoubtedly part of the backdrop to Keats's flourishing art. Galileo Galilei (1564-1642) could only have found the moons of Jupiter by looking into Copernicus's (1473-1543) telescope. Similarly, the teenage

Keats found, thanks to Chapman's translation, hitherto un-glimpsed beauty, but – and this is one thing that makes Keats's contribution to modern thought so challenging and distinctive – he allowed that beauty to continue to exist on its own other-worldly terms without trying to haul it with Herculean disrespect into the light of common day. That is, the 'swimming' new 'planet' was not suddenly taken out of its twilit element of dreams and poetry and then fatally reduced by the eyes and understanding at the waking, worldly end of the 'telescope'. Denis Diderot (1713-84) may have proclaimed influentially in the *Encyclopedia, or a systematic dictionary of the sciences, arts, and crafts* (1745-1772) that 'all things must be examined, debated, investigated without exception and without regard for anyone's feelings' and that 'We must ride roughshod over all these ancient puerilities, overturn the barriers that reason never erected', but Keats was not to use any new 'planet' (or any of his other discoveries) to rattle any Ptolemaic or medieval paradigm. Just as he was not really all that interested in Hazlitt's and Hunt's visions of political revolution, so too he was not really all that interested in the Copernican revolution. More captivatingly, he offers the reader a view *in* (' ... to Chapman's Homer') to the great mystery, rather than *out* at an alienating propinquity of 'realities'. The great mystery's real locus, for Keats, is like, though not literally, 'the Pacific' ocean, sparkling and yearning (as humans sparkle and yearn), and teeming with unknown modes of being (as humans teem). 'There will,' said Hunt in an article that praised Keats to the skies, 'be a poetry of the imagination, as long as the first causes of things remain a mystery.' (*Indicator*, August 1820)

By this point in his quest, his pilgrimage to higher realms of soul and spirit (having already that year, 1816, decided not to pursue medicine as a career), the poet found expression for his apprehension just before, and his transformation during, psychic discovery. (At the same time, he found expression for his apprehension about his first real look at high culture.) He was getting to know himself in a way, and at a depth, that few do.

Having been given Bonnycastle's *Introduction to Astronomy* in 1811, he would have read about William Herschel's (1738-1822) discovery of Uranus 35 years earlier, and he possibly attended Charles Babbage's (1792-1871) 1815 'Lectures on Astronomy' at the Royal Institution. Keats saw the point of science. He did not, however, see why, or even how, it could be driven through the irregular aliveness of Psyche (to use the ancient Grecians' term for soul's symbol) without regularising and wasting it. An actual, external, remote entity like Europa, or Uranus, no longer 'swims' 'like a gentle whispering/Of all the secrets of some wondrous thing/That breathes about us in the vacant air' (*Sleep and Poetry*, 29-31) once scientists have fished it out of its celestial provenance and into the interests of reason and progress. Keats is not interested in looking literally into the bowl of a telescope. He wants to see past the hundred percent bleakness of lumps in space to what they symbolise: 'we look around with prying stare,/Perhaps to see shapes of light, aerial limning,/And catch soft floatings from a faint-heard hymning ... ' (*Sleep and Poetry*, 32-4). In a letter to Haydon, he would discuss 'looking upon the Sun the Moon the stars, the Earth and its contents as materials to form greater things – that is to say ethereal things' (*Letters*, I, p.143). This is very different to, say, Herschel's son's cataloguing of well over 500 nebulae and star clusters.

Chapman's verse translation of Homer's *Iliad* helped Keats to get acquainted with this vital, yet neglected, mode of vision at its most powerful: 'Like rich Autumnus' golden lampe, whose brightness men admire,/Past all the other host of Starres, when with his cheerful face,/Fresh washt in lofty Ocean waves, he doth his Skies enchase.' (Book 5) Keats is contemplating, not counting (as Homer and Chapman contemplated, rather than counted, the 'host of Starres'). The comparison of the golden glow of the Greek warrior Diomed's helmet with the glow of the planet Jupiter rising above the sea in autumn is one of the moments in Chapman's Homer that most excited Keats. Clarke, to whom Hunt probably lent a 1616 folio edition of Chapman's translation, remembered that the poet 'sometimes shouted' on hearing certain passages recited during 'a memorable night' (probably during the weekend of 11 to 12 October, 1816, in Clerkenwell), after which Keats left Clarke at 6 am, and went home with the music of the spheres – and one of the finest works of antiquity – ringing in his head. By 10 am, a postal messenger had delivered Keats's sonnet to Clarke.

Keats's opinion that his beloved Thomas Chatterton's (1752-70) 'medieval' idiom showed him to be 'the purest writer in the English language' is significant: the first six lines of 'On First Looking into Chapman's Homer' are characterised by antiquated words such as 'bards', 'demesne' and 'fealty', and the speaker has, as he archaically puts it, 'many goodly states and kingdoms seen'. The poem goes on to express something of a purer (more medieval) way of experiencing the heavens – but in an age of hot air balloons, steam engines and the increasing extent of artificial light in buildings and on streets, contemporary readers were tending to esteem works (and themselves) when they were underpinned by science and utility, and so readers were seeing medievalism in pejorative terms that brought to mind benightedness and *impurity* best sloughed off.

The magical images of the medieval epoch had haunted the human mind luminously and voluminously (Milton's *Paradise Lost* is the last great literary powerhouse of such images) until the decisive cuts of the Enlightenment lancet, and then the mentality of lettered Europe was disinfected from the top down by French intellectualism, through the Industrial Revolution, to the nihilism of the later nineteenth century, right through to the ultra-nihilism of the twentieth century. Our universe is now pitch-black and empty, but for the unaccountable mess of stars and statistics. There's no one here, we're told. We're disabled. We're helpless. We might cultivate a special way of being alone, or a special way of being afraid, but the predicament is no different whined at than withstood. Deep down, we know this is an inadequate apprehension of reality. Keats peoples the vacancy with his animating sincerity:

> O come! let us haste to the freshening shades,
> The quaintly carv'd seats, and the opening glades;
> Where the faeries are chanting their evening hymns,
> And in the last sun-beam the sylph lightly swims. ('To Emma')

The imaginary being once assumed to inhabit the air ('the sylph') is not to be reeled as it really is into the bright, hard light of new, clarity-seeking humans. It is not to be pinned as it really is on a cork, its wings outspread. It is not to become, literally, a specimen in a box covered with glass, hung on a wall, and filled with other dead sylphs, as a collection: Keats was one of the key English writers who effectively opposed the secularisation that would dragoon succeeding generations of men and women through a peculiarly punishing era of psychological hygiene.

Hazlitt's Romantic maxim could be a fitting epitaph for Keats, if one is unaware of the routine subjection of the poet and his beloved siblings to the innumerable petty miseries of not having much money, and not having many connections: 'Happy are they who live in the dream of their own existence, and see all things in the light of their own minds; who walk by faith and hope; to whom the guiding star of their youth still shines from afar, and into whom the spirit of the world has not yet entered. The world has no hand on them.' 'The world', if one wants to 'get on' in it, too often puts one in the invidious position of having to be untrue to oneself. While the efforts of aristocrats such as Byron and Shelley were often seen to have an authority informed by their conviction of having the right to be entirely themselves, the efforts of cockneys were often seen as contemptibly helpless because they were 'unacquainted' with anywhere except 'the neighbourhood of London' (as 'Z', with his well-bred brevity, tact, loftiness and malice, evoked the arrogance and ignorance of London's scarcely-travelled, semi-literate little citizens). Keats's brother George probably illustrated a lower-middle class truism – truthfulness is next to joblessness – on having to give up his position at Richard Abbey's counting-house due to a disagreement with Abbey's junior partner, Cadman Hodgkinson (slightly senior to George), whom John hated. It is a perilous business, when one has been orphaned and impoverished, to neglect to pay the daily psychic cost involved in parrying and distributing throughout the workplace the various counterpointing moods of one's better-connected co-workers.

Nevertheless, the paper on which there may at one time have been a record of the quarrel between George Keats and Cadman Hodgkinson has probably since passed through the intestines of a long-deceased rat, and Hazlitt's words can therefore with ultimate justice celebrate Keats's separateness from the age – as characteristic of an alternative world-view (whose lineage may be traced back to Plato) for which the majority of any given generation since the Enlightenment has always been clever and keen enough to point out the absence of empirical evidence.

Now widely regarded as Keats's first great sonnet, 'On First Looking into Chapman's Homer' is replete with a melting variability of mental realities: four lines from the end of the poem, the narrator is no longer like 'some watcher of the skies', but 'like stout Cortez', the Spanish conquistador who discovered and defeated the Aztecs, and conquered Mexico in 1523. Motion points out that Keats 'mistakes Balboa … for Cortez, and so undermines [his] air of learning.' Pointing out, also, that the poet 'succumbs to a moment of awkward translationese ("pure serene") which creates a sense of Keats standing apart from the main event' (Motion, p.112), Motion reveals that his vantage-point as Keats's biographer is situated somewhere between admiration and vindictiveness. There are many strains on a writer's sympathies when he fastens for some years his attention on another writer's life and work. But when that biographer, whose sympathies are being strained (in the 1990s), is the poet who wrote *The Pleasure Steamers* in his mid-20s and the biographee is the teenage writer of 'On First Looking into Chapman's Homer', the exercise will inevitably resolve itself into yet another overlong record of a non-meeting of minds. The ubiquity of this sort of asymmetry, and the endless provision of mere literary distraction as though for readers in need of it, continues to put people off – or at any rate keep people from – actually reading the great poetry itself. When Val Hennessy told *Daily Mail* readers that 'Motion possesses a hotline to Keats in heaven', she was soliciting the low-middlebrow sunniness in which sincerity vaporises before becoming big enough to bore. And Edmund White, who championed Motion's 'restored' and 'glowing' Keats in the *Observer* would confess some years later in his freehand memoir, *City Boy* (2009), just how craven and untrue to himself he had been many times as a book reviewer.

Keats knew that his dreams and their sequent poems enact variants of his conscious life. (The best readers of Keats know that their dreams enact variants of their conscious lives.) The mention of Darien may remind one of the disastrous attempt to establish a Scottish colony there in 1698, and if one conjectures (or perhaps dreams) about the possible sequence of events and personal circumstances that brought, say, the third (or the tenth, or the twelfth) speculator to the point of setting foot on the vessel that would sail for the Caribbean, one begins to unfold, as it were, the leaves of a close-folded latitude of imagination quite beyond the ken of Keats's reviewer contemporaries, and his later biographers (and their reviewer contemporaries).

In one way, the poet is evolving at a depth where only a kind of salamander could apprehend what really goes on in the meeting waters of dreams and poetry – 'like … gems upcurl'd/In the recesses of a pearly shell' (*Sleep and Poetry*, 121-22). In another way – in the sense of alchemical achievement – the poet mired previously in politics is transforming himself. In the later poem, *Endymion*, he will postulate a time when 'we shine,/Full alchemiz'd, and free of space.' (I, 779-80) Either way, the 'realms of gold' into which Keats is initiated – by way of Homer's echoes through the centuries, and involving, further, Chapman's own insightful cadences – are richly and immediately applicable: 'His [Neptune's] bright and glorious palace built, of never-rusting gold;/And there arriv'd, he put in Coach, his brazen-footed steeds,/All golden man'd, and pac't with wings; and all in golden weeds/He cloth'd himself.' (Book 13)

The fascinated astronomer, or the rapacious European invader – or the journalist scrambling for copy – may have found sensational discoveries, but he himself is not transformed, even as, for example, Bottom was by Titania's beauty, let alone by the Divine. Despite the Enlightenment, and Europe's subsequent stress on the importance of reason and the critical reappraisal of existing ideas and institutions, Keats still feels worshipful in the presence of the night sky. Indeed, he feels worshipful in the presence of anything from the primary source of light in the whole planetary system to one of the countless little lives on earth it makes possible: 'The setting sun will always set me to rights – or if a Sparrow come before my Window I take part in its existence and pick about the Gravel.' (*Letters*, I, p.186) He knows his contribution to thought will not involve his resolving, with technologically enhanced eyesight, say, the Milky Way into a 'correct' answer. He knows that the 'problem' cannot be solved because it is not a problem – it is a mystery, but not the kind of mystery to be approached, let alone handled, by state-funded philosophers. 'The Genius of Poetry must work out its own salvation in a man: It cannot be matured by law & precept, but by sensation & watchfulness in itself – That which is creative must create itself' (*Letters*, I, p.374). He knows that his concern is, at one and the same time, with the timeless vision and the all-too-visible facts of our base world. He knows that he must live without resolutions in a state of creative tension. The beautiful and terrible energies of life will frequently divulge confidences to him. He feels right through him the weight – or, perhaps, the lightness Milan Kundera (1929-) will call unbearable – of the responsibility to keep up the correspondence. He will not be able to make these confidences less vague, or more easily handled, merely by thinking harder. He will not abandon his quest in despair. He will stay in the storm on his own terms, however perplexingly the world carries on: 'let us not … go hurrying about and collecting honey-bee like, buzzing here and there impatiently from a knowledge of what is to be arrived at: but let us open our leaves like a flower and be passive and receptive – budding patiently under the eye of Apollo and taking hints from every noble insect that favors us with a visit … ' (*Letters*, I, p.232). Despite his purpose as a writer – revelation, or apocalypse – he knows, as his most insightful contemporaries know, that the very words he employs can limit his efforts: 'one cannot write a wink, or a nod, or a grin, or a purse of the Lips, or a *smile – O law!* One can-[not] put one's finger to one's nose, or yerk ye in the ribs, or lay hold of your button in writing' (*Letters*, II, p.205). There is always the possibility of failing to transmit the full value of one's thoughts to the page. Keats was not the only Romantic writer to be concerned about this. In his Introduction to his paraphrased translation of Plotinus's (205?-270? AD) essay 'Concerning the Beautiful' (1787), Thomas Taylor (1758-1835) had already said 'It may seem wonderful that language, which is the only method of conveying our conceptions, should, at the same time, be a hindrance to our advancement in philosophy.' Coleridge often felt that his ideas flourished most felicitously amongst the contingencies of spontaneous utterance, and when Hazlitt spitefully accused him of being more of a talker than a doer, he reduced Coleridge to the heat of bygone performances, to the vanished intimacies of particular occasions. 'If a man could pass through Paradise in a dream,' thought Coleridge, 'and have a flower presented to him as a pledge that his soul had really been there, and if he found that flower in his hand when he awoke – Aye! and what then?' (*Coleridge Notebooks*, 4287) Keats thought and wrote in a manner cultivated to promote the unforced flourishing of dream flowers. Alfred Tennyson (1809-92) would later write in his long poem, *In Memoriam* (1850), that 'words, like Nature, half reveal/And half conceal the Soul within.' Keats feels simultaneously turned on, and put off, by the sacrifice and struggle involved in generating the written word as illumination: 'I began [*Endymion*] about a Fortnight since and have done some every day except travelling ones – Perhaps I may have done a good deal for the time but it appears such a Pin's Point to me that I will not copy any out – When I consider that so many of these Pin points go to form a Bodkin point … and that it requ[i]res a thousand bodkins to make a Spear bright enough to throw any light to posterity – I see that nothing but continual uphill Journeying?' (*Letters*, I, p.139) As Keats sends his gaze right into 'Paradise', or 'a dream', or the dark, trying to remember always to dilate rather than squint, it is almost as if the last sentence quoted above succumbs to some third law of grammatical dynamics. The questionable question mark, like a surprise spot of arterial blood on a handkerchief, might signal the beginning of an individual's transformation into something higher – signalling an imminent inrush of insight from beyond the brink of syntax. When he finds himself, one might say, beside himself with anxiety or confusion, he lets the personal doubleness – just as he lets the planet, or the sylph – run its course, or dance its dance, or be whatever it really is, or do whatever it really does, because he knows what the Roman historian and statesman, Sallust (86-?34 BC), knew: 'These things never happened; they are always.'

Keats felt the weight of the same mystery that burdened the ancient Romans, the ancient Greeks, Dante (1265-1321), Shakespeare, and the great contemporary writers such as Wordsworth and Coleridge. He felt his soul, as they felt their souls. He felt, as they theirs felt, his own soul's vital connection with the mystery. He knew that a metaphorical amputation of his soul from the mystery would be worse for him than no effort to deal with the situation at all. He knew not to try to manage things by attempting even a temporary separation of soul from mystery. Yet without lightness of some kind he would achieve nothing. Without blind Enlightenment, however, couldn't he achieve something great? In the Preface to *Foliage*, Hunt said that Shakespeare, 'felt the Grecian mythology not as a set of schoolboy common-places which it was thought wrong to give out, but as something which it requires more than mere scholarship to understand – as the elevation of the external world … to the highest pitch of the graceful, and as embodied essences of all the grand and lovely qualities of nature.' Keats could not read the actual words of Homer or Archimedes (?287-212 BC), but he appreciated what Hunt called 'the deepest taste of antiquity' to be found in plays like *A Winter's Tale* and *The Tempest*. On first looking into Chapman's Homer, Keats found himself on the edge of eureka, dizzy with déjà vu. No wonder he shouted. If the surviving members of the Keats family could be pushed around in the neighbourhood of London, John Keats had caught sight of a new neighbourhood in which the usual oppressors would have no say-so.

3

Endymion: A Poetic Romance

Having seen visionary truth through the slight gap in the fabric of life created by the 14 lines of 'On First Looking into Chapman's Homer', Keats wanted to prolong the vision in an epic poem. He wanted to 'make 4000 Lines of one bare circumstance and fill them with Poetry' (*Letters*, I, p.170). He knew at heart, however, that he would try, and fail, to produce a work with that uniformity of impression that distinguishes, say, Milton's *Paradise Lost* (in which the sensual, the sexual, the spiritual and the political are made somehow to achieve the synergism of a single, epic insight from the other side of time), because he knew that he (unlike Milton) worked in fits and starts. 'I can only write in scraps and patches'.

Endymion did present the metropolitan wits with plenty of easy targets for criticism. In inscribing the poem to the memory of Chatterton – the boy poet of 'low' origins who faked 'medieval' poems, and after discovery killed himself – Keats was all but asking for trouble. In the poem itself, there are, as Shelley told Keats in a letter dated 27 July 1820, 'treasures … though poured forth with indistinct profusion. This, people in general will not endure'. Here is an example of the kind of half-alchemised imagery that Shelley thought 'people' would 'not endure':

> Love's madness he had known:
> Often with more than tortured lion's groan
> Moanings had burst from him; but now that rage
> Had pass'd away: no longer did he wage
> A rough-voic'd war against the dooming stars.
> No, he had felt too much for such harsh jars:
> The lyre of his soul Æolian tun'd
> Forgot all violence, and but commun'd
> With melancholy thought: O he had swoon'd
> Drunken from pleasure's nipple … (*Endymion*, II, 860-9).

Even that great essayist, opium-eater and appreciator of poetic dreamscapes, Thomas De Quincey (1785-1859), so hugely impressed by Keats's later poetry, referred to *Endymion* as 'the very midsummer madness of affectation.' (*Works of Thomas De Quincey*, ed. Lindop, Vol. 15, p.307) Motion has been struck by the number of times in *Endymion* that the hero 'confuses sexual longing with the need to be mothered', the number of times love is described 'as a nourishing drink', and the amount of time the hero spends 'gazing at women's breasts' (Motion, p.42). It is taking Keats rather a long time to outgrow this particular fascination. In 'Hadst thou liv'd in days of old' (1817), he keeps returning to 'those beauties, scarce discern'd,/Kept with such sweet privacy,/That they seldom meet the eye' and 'the silver sheen/Of thy broider'd floating vest/Cov'ring half thine ivory breast …/Keeping secret what is fair.' And still, in the passage from *Endymion* above, the hero appears to be whimpering like a tormented lion, yet quaffing something medicinal from the teat of an abstract noun.

There is something cluttered and incomplete about much of *Endymion*. It may be discerned that the writer has dared to believe that he is destined to undergo, realise and express higher states of consciousness. There is perhaps a want of humility and even simplicity in the writing (though something's being simple does not necessarily, as Keats knows, mean that it is not complicated). Perhaps if the writer was simpler and more natural it would be easier for him to accept this. Who does he think he is? The following, from a letter to Bailey, shows what he thinks he is: 'Men of Genius are great as certain ethereal Chemicals operating on the Mass of neutral intellect – b[ut] they have not any individuality, any determined Character.' In the same letter, he shows what he does not think he is: 'I would call the top and head of those who have a proper self Men of Power.' (*Letters*, I, p.184) He is not interested in being a Man of Power. And he is not interested enough in developing in himself the quick, corrupt, sophisticated intelligence more likely to make a journalist or an academic than a poet. The journalistic or academic kind of intelligence is an enemy of the imaginative fluency inseparable from Keats's greatness, and it would only prevent the poet's development by cleverly making that fluency seem reckless. 'In Endymion, I leaped headlong into the Sea, and thereby have become better acquainted with the Soundings, the quicksands, & the rocks, than if I had stayed upon the green shore, and piped a silly pipe, and took tea & comfortable advice. – I was never afraid of failure; for I would sooner fail than not be among the greatest' (*Letters*, I, p.374).

Endymion was Keats's first long poem, and he wanted it to be 'a regular stepping of the Imagination towards a Truth.' (*Letters*, I, p.218) He wanted to prove to his friends, the public, and himself that he could retell classical myth in a sustained and independent way. But there was a problem, and it was a very big one at the time: he had no Greek. At this point in his career, Keats was more demonstrably indebted to Hunt's *Story of Rimini* (1816), with all its highly wrought, digressive splendour, than he was to any of the great writers of antiquity:

> The sun is up, and 'tis a morn of May
> Round old Ravenna's clear-shewn towers and bay,
> A morn, the loveliest which the year has seen,
> Last of the spring, yet fresh with all its green;
> For a warm eve, and gentle rains at night,
> Have left a sparkling welcome for the light,
> And there's a crystal clearness all about;
> The leaves are sharp, the distant hills look out;
> A balmy briskness comes upon the breeze;
> And smoke goes dancing from the cottage trees;
> And when you listen, you may hear a coil
> Of bubbling springs about the grassy soil;
> And all the scene, in short – sky, earth and sea,
> Breathes like a bright-eyed face, that laughs but openly.

(The Story of Rimini, Canto I)

In his sonnet, 'On Leigh Hunt's Poem "The Story of Rimini"', Keats again venerates Hunt's 'region of his own' and his 'bower for his spirit' in a way that suggests Keats aspires to *his* own 'region' and *his* own 'bower'. At the time of writing and publishing *Endymion*, Keats seemed to hope that readers would be able to enjoy enough light from his fitful insightfulness, and even be able to make out the contours of a maturity (and even a Miltonic consistency) not yet realised: 'The imagination of a boy is healthy, and the mature imagination of a man is healthy; but there is a space of life between, in which the soul is in ferment, the character undecided, the way of life uncertain, the ambition thick-sighted: thence proceeds mawkishness, and all the thousand bitters which those men I speak of must necessarily taste in going over the following pages.' (Preface, *Endymion*) In traversing the 'ferment' between boy- and man-hood, the poet (argues the poet) is forced to produce the excrescences that he fears will rob, for many readers, the scattered jewels of their shine.

Keats was also indebted to *Alastor* (1815), in which Shelley had recreated the raptness of youthful poets so beautifully and powerfully –

> Oh, that the dream
> Of dark magician in his visioned cave,
> Raking the cinders of a crucible
> For life and power, even when his feeble hand
> Shakes in its last decay, were the true law
> Of this so lovely world! (*Alastor*, 681-6)

– with a view to criticising it. Shelley had the same painful knowledge as Keats that the light of common day would disinterestedly excoriate the dreamer on his return. Shelley's lament, 'But thou art fled,/Like some frail exhalation, which the dawn/Robes in its golden beams, – ah! thou hast fled!' (*Alastor*, 686-8), is echoed in Keats's *Sleep and Poetry*:

> The visions all are fled – the car is fled
> Into the light of heaven, and in their stead
> As sense of real things comes doubly strong,
> And, like a muddy stream, would bear along
> My soul to nothingness … (*Sleep and Poetry*, 155-9).

In *Alastor*, Shelley, a 23-year-old aristocrat, had diagnosed solitary idealism as the root of an unhappiness in himself and in Britain (assuming in the latter, national form an insularity that considers anything not the product of British effort to be a sort of moral error). Perhaps the teenager writing *Sleep and Poetry* and *Endymion* – divided from, and coveting, the rank of the classically educated – was conscious of a vulgarity (not just an immaturity) about his idea of a poet's resolve. Perhaps he worried that it was already too late for the deficit of sophistication to be made good. Adults, even brand new ones, who tamper publicly with their inherited limitations are likely to be singled out for scorn. Henry Stephens, the author of *Edwi and Elgiba*, recalled the 'pride and conceit' of the medical student whose real ambition was to be a great poet: 'In [our sitting room] he was always at the window, peering into space, so that the window-seat was spoken of by his comrades as Keats's place … In the lecture room he seemed to sit apart and be absorbed in something else, as if the subject suggested thoughts to him which were not practically connected with it. He was often in the subject and out of it, in a dreamy way.' Countless individuals have behaved like this before and since Keats, and it may easily be imagined that such behaviour is usually, once spotted, considered groundless. Who among the vulgar multitude cares about the misery of unfulfilled imagination? Keats recalled 'the kirkmen' who did 'Scotland harm' by banishing the joyous impulses that lead to poetry, and he recalled the predicament of a poet – Robert Burns (1759-96) – with whom he could empathise: 'Poor unfortunate fellow, how sad it is when a luxurious imagination is obliged in self-defence to deaden its delicacy in vulgarity' (*Letters*, I, pp.319-20). Henry Stephens's account of Keats seems to depend on how it is read – does the reader recognise in the following words a favourable recollection of a young poet's uniqueness, or some irony on behalf of the non-poetic majority? 'He never attached much consequence to his own studies in medicine, and indeed looked upon the medical career as the career by which to live in a workaday world, without being certain that he could keep up the strain of it. He nevertheless had a consciousness of his own powers, and even of his own greatness, though it might never be recognised … '.

How the poet makes his way through the tirelessly-manned Hades of ordinary life can determine the quality of the respect he can confer upon himself before he can consider himself capable of transmuting base matters into realms of gold.

> Poetry was to his mind a zenith of all his Aspirations: the only thing worth the attention of superior minds: so he thought: all other pursuits were mean and tame … The greatest men in the world were the poets and to rank among them was the chief object of his ambition. It may readily be imagined that this feeling was accompanied with a good deal of pride and conceit, and that amongst mere medical students he would walk and talk as one of the gods might be supposed to do when mingling with mortals. This pride exposed him, as may readily be imagined, to occasional ridicule, and some mortification. (Stephens quoted in Motion, p.91)

Stephens's pen portrait of Keats could be of any individual member of the lower middle classes ostentatiously polishing his supposedly secret angel-wings, and it could put one in mind, perhaps, of George Bernard Shaw's (1856-1950) definition, in his 'Maxims for Revolutionists' (from *Man and Superman*, 1903), of greatness ('only one of the sensations of littleness'), or of Robert Walser's (1878-1956) short story about Helbling, convinced of his inner fineness in comparison to his co-workers (though apparently unaware that he is merely a representative member of one division of humanity as lacking and tedious as any other). To critics of Keats – Marjorie Levinson is an excellent example – animated in the broad frame of reference enriched by intellectuals like Shaw and Walser (not to mention erected in the first place by Freud and Marx), Keats's self-fashioning can look familiarly strenuous:

> … but I will strive
> Against all doubtings, and will keep alive
> The thought of that same chariot, and the strange
> Journey it went (*Sleep and Poetry*, 159-62).

And yet in many of his utterances Keats can seem to share more in common with Sir Walter Scott's (1771-1832) Edward Waverley (so sensible of his own want of finish) than with Cervantes's (1547-1616) Don Quixote (so flawlessly deluded):

> There were a few other youths of better education, and a more liberal character; but from their society … our hero was in some degree excluded … The idea of having committed the slightest solecism in politeness, whether real or imaginary, was agony to him; for perhaps even guilt itself does not impose upon some minds so keen a sense of shame and remorse, as a modest, sensitive and inexperienced youth feels from the consciousness of having neglected etiquette, or excited ridicule. Where we are not at ease, we cannot be happy; and therefore it is not surprising, that Edward Waverley supposed that he disliked and was unfitted for society, merely because he had not yet acquired the habit of living in it with ease and comfort … (*Waverley*, Chapter 4).

Keats's self-image wavered. On one day (for example, 14 October 1818) he could be convinced that he would be among the English poets after his death. On another day, in a different mood, he may have remembered Francis Beaumont (1584-1616) and John Fletcher's (1579-1625) play, *Philaster, or Love Lies-Ableeding* (1611) – 'All your better deeds/Shall be in water writ' (V, 3) – and become so sure that his own name might just as well have been written in water that he would ask his friend Joseph Severn (1793-1879) to have the words 'Here lies one whose name was writ in water' inscribed on his gravestone. He often worried that anything he could ever write would always have something inadequate and even insulting about it to readers who knew better. However, the worry did not render him perpetually costive, as his Preface to *Endymion* shows: 'This may be speaking too presumptuously, and may deserve a punishment: but no feeling man will be forward to inflict it: he will leave me alone, with the conviction that there is not a fiercer hell than the failure in a great object. This is not written with the least atom of purpose to forestall criticisms of course, but from the desire I have to conciliate men who are competent to look, and who do look with a zealous eye, to the honour of English literature.' (Preface, *Endymion*) Just as deprivation was to Philip Larkin (1922-85) what daffodils were to Wordsworth, so Keats had his uncertainties.

Byron had first introduced himself to the British public via his preface to *Hours of Idleness* (1807). The effortless arrogance of Byron's entreaty not to be indulged in reviews on account of his nobility turned the reviewers against him. Now, in Keats, it was lower-middle-class humility – so unsure of itself and so easily fobbed off or made an example of – that was catapulting a new poet into unpopularity. The Preface to *Endymion* is shot through with the author's inordinate appeals to the kindness of strangers, and – worse – it is imbued with his servile love of the light in which he knew he would stand condemned: 'I hope I have not in too late a day touched the beautiful mythology of Greece, and dulled its brightness: for I wish to try once more, before I bid it farewell.' (Preface, *Endymion*) This statement has in it both the presumption and timidity that can sound to the 'higher orders' so typical of the overtures made to them by the 'lower orders'. In his lines 'Written on a Blank Space at the End of Chaucer's Tale of "The Floure and the Leafe"' (1817), Keats announces himself as 'I that do ever feel a thirst for glory', but a month later he feels the need to apologise to his classically-informed friend, Haydon, for his own exclusively intuitive appreciation of a piece of great art that they had viewed together:

> Haydon! Forgive me that I cannot speak
> Definitively on these mighty things;
> Forgive me that I have not Eagle's wings –
> That what I want I know not where to seek …
> ('To Haydon With a Sonnet Written on Seeing the Elgin Marbles').

Keats self-deprecatingly, diplomatically, and disarmingly regards his own Greeklessness as a disability:

> My spirit is too weak – Mortality
> Weighs heavily on me like unwilling sleep,
> And each imagined pinnacle and steep
> Of godlike hardship, tells me I must die
> Like a sick Eagle looking at the sky. ('On Seeing the Elgin Marbles', 1817)

Haydon responded with opulent sympathy: 'I know not a finer image than the comparison of a Poet unable to express his high feelings to a sick eagle looking at the Sky!' Just as Coleridge had been paradoxically strengthened by his sense of weakness in 'Dejection: an ode' (1802), so Keats was writing with a view to remaining poetically capable when in the grip of negative emotions.

The best passages of *Endymion* illustrate the longevity, rather than the frailty, of poetic exaltation:

> Nor do we merely feel these essences
> For one short hour; no, even as the trees
> That whisper round a temple become soon
> Dear as the temple's self, so does the moon,
> The passion poesy, glories infinite,
> Haunt us till they become a cheering light
> Unto our souls ... (I, 25-31).

Furthermore, for the poet, 'these essences' do not merely shine 'Unto our souls', but they are, more vitally, 'bound to us so fast,/That, whether there be shine, or gloom o'ercast,/They always must be with us, or we die.' (I, 31-3) In other words, the world in which one moves and thinks has been put there by the power of poetry. And once it has been put there, it cannot be taken away:

> A thing of beauty is a joy for ever:
> Its loveliness increases; it will never
> Pass into nothingness; but still will keep
> A bower quiet for us, and a sleep
> Full of sweet dreams ... (I, 1-5).

In order to produce such pearls, the young poet takes life to heart (or lets himself be taken to life's heart), convolving himself in an intensity of 'self-indulgence' and 'narcissism' easily identified by those trained to weed unguarded emotions out of themselves, that they may mount and melt into the upper air of bourgeois indifference.

Endymion is replete with proliferations of overlapping problems. The verbal and conceptual undergrowth could be picked over with fascinated yet ill-disposed exactitude. (The fact that some of Keats's unkindest critics took care not to be seen to do this may have made them look reasonably well-disposed and magnanimous even as they condemned the poem, and the poet. This approach, as any experienced bully knows, is a stock-in-trade one with which to hoot the victim out of town.) Sometimes, for example, the poet's forced impostures in reaching for the word that rhymes, and the concomitantly higgledy-piggledy syllable-count look temporary – as if they'll have to do for now:

> I clung about her waist, nor ceas'd to pass
> Fleet as an arrow through unfathom'd brine,
> Until there shone a fabric crystalline,
> Ribb'd and inlaid with coral, pebble, and pearl. (III, 626-9)

Keats had already made clear – be it remembered – his desire for readers to tolerate (if not endorse) any shabbiness about the appearance of the poem:

> What manner I mean, will be quite clear to the reader, who must soon perceive … every error denoting a feverish attempt, rather than a deed accomplished. The two first books, and indeed the two last, I feel sensible are not of such completion as to warrant their passing the press; nor should they if I thought a year's castigation would do them any good; – it will not: the foundations are too sandy. It is just that this youngster should die away: a sad thought for me, if I had not some hope that while it is dwindling I may be plotting, and fitting myself for verses fit to live. (Preface, *Endymion*)

Shelley did recognise the poem as a harbinger of 'the greatest things' from Keats. However, in the meantime, Keats had to make his way despised. One can imagine the satisfaction of Keats's (and Hunt's) enemies on first encountering *Endymion*'s outbreaks of narrative confusion and naivety.

The Tory politician John Wilson Croker (1780-1857) and the prominent supporter of Tory politics, John Gibson Lockhart (1794-1854) – the 'Z' of the *Blackwood's* series of articles, 'The Cockney School of Poetry' – denounced *Endymion* with predictable relish. 'I shall have the reputation of Hunt's élève,' Keats told Bailey. Here is an excerpt from Croker's anonymous review in the September 1818 *Quarterly*:

> This author is a copyist of Mr Hunt, but he is more unintelligible, almost as rugged, twice as diffuse, and ten times more tiresome and absurd than his prototype, who, though he impudently presumed to seat himself in the chair of criticism, and to measure his own poetry by his own standard, yet generally had a meaning. But Mr Keats had advanced no dogmas which he was bound to support by examples; his nonsense therefore is quite gratuitous; he writes for his own sake, and, being bitten by Mr Hunt's insane criticism, more than rivals the insanity of his poetry … (*Keats: Narrative Poetry*, p.43).

For Croker, Keats is the deep and meaningless Cockney romantic – the all-dreaming, non-thinking imitator of the egregious King of the Cockneys, Hunt.

The thunderhead of judgment was slower to gather in Lockhart's *Blackwood's* review (August 1818), and his armour-plated eighteenth-century class-sensibility remained intact as he furnished his readers with his survey of Britain's cultural decline in general, before introducing Keats as a mere symptom of that decline:

> Of all the manias of this mad age, the most incurable, as well as the most common, seems to be no other than the *Metromanie*. The just celebrity of Robert Burns and Miss Baillie has had the melancholy effect of turning the heads of we know not how many farm-servants and unmarried ladies; our very footmen compose tragedies, and there is scarcely a superannuated governess in the island that does not leave a roll of lyrics behind her in her band-box. (*Keats: Narrative Poetry*, p.41.)

For Lockhart, Keats (who had become eligible to practise as an apothecary, physician and surgeon in July 1816) was of little higher origin than a farm-servant or a footman, stomping through the thoughts of finer sensibilities heavily and unseeingly. Having drolly portrayed a whiffling century in which anyone fancying himself winged with the poetic impulse could get into print, Lockhart alerted readers to Keats's misapplication of his 'potentially professional' (though never literary) talents:

> This young man appears to have received from nature talents of an excellent, perhaps even of a superior order – talents which, devoted to the purposes of any useful profession, must have rendered him a respectable, if not an eminent citizen. His friends, we understand, destined him to the career of medicine, and he was bound apprentice some years ago to a worthy apothecary in town. But all has been undone by a sudden attack of the malady to which we have alluded. Whether Mr John has been sent home with a diuretic or composing draught to some patient far gone in the poetical mania, we have not heard. This much is certain, that he has caught the infection, and that thoroughly. (*Keats: Narrative Poetry*, p.41)

Finally, after breaking into mock earnestness and appearing to deliver a home-truth personally to the talented (though, it had to be affirmed, barbarian and bold) young man, Lockhart ushered him to the outskirts of high culture, and put his trust in the unlikelihood of such an unrefined newcomer surviving the conditions of peripherality: 'It is a better and a wiser thing to be a starved apothecary than a starved poet; so back to the shop Mr John, back to the "plasters, pills, ointment boxes", &c. But, for Heaven's sake, young Sangrado, be a little more sparing of extenuatives and soporifics in your practice than you have been in your poetry.' (*Keats: Narrative Poetry*, p.41)

In 1820, a year before Keats's death, an unsigned review in the *London Magazine* said that Keats's 'knowledge of Greek and Mythology seem[ed] to mystify him on every occasion'. Keats had no university education at all, and for his harshest critics he was guilty of something unforgivably plebeian: though he was 'without Greek', he still had the effrontery 'to talk about the gods'. In short, he was just another Londoner with pretensions (and an inexcusably reform-minded track record).

Francis Jeffrey (1773-1850), editor of the *Edinburgh Review* (1803-29), appeared to some extent to keep his attitude to Keats aloof and chilly:

Even in the judgment of a fitter audience, however, it must, we fear, be admitted, that, beside the riot and extravagance of his fancy, the scope and substance of Mr Keats's poetry is rather too dreamy and abstracted to excite the strongest interest, or to sustain the attention through a work of any great compass or extent. He deals too much with shadowy and incomprehensible beings, and is too constantly rapt into an extramundane Elysium, to command a lasting interest with ordinary mortals, and must employ the agency of more varied and coarser emotions, if he wishes to take rank with the enduring poets of this or of former generations.

What could better flatter the complacency of ignorance than a piece of literary criticism expressing concern about an author's hazy indifference to terrestrial matters and inability to condescend to 'coarser emotions'? Having already, more than once, in the interests of 'the public good', savaged the radical Wordsworth in print, Jeffrey was a more experienced defender of Britain than the 23-year-old Lockhart. However, Jeffrey still concluded his review of Keats by effectively corroborating Lockhart's analysis of the 'rising brood of Cockneys', those fundamentally doltish farm-helpers, footmen and apothecaries with ambitions, but insufficient classical education, to produce poetry for 'ordinary [classically educated] mortals' to read: 'Mr Keats has unquestionably a very beautiful imagination, a perfect ear for harmony, and a great familiarity with the finest diction of English poetry; but he must learn not to misuse or misapply these advantages; and neither to waste the good gifts of Nature and study on intractable themes, nor to luxuriate too recklessly on such as are more suitable.' (*Edinburgh Review*, XXXIV, August 1820) If Croker and Lockhart – whom Hazlitt called 'the talking potato' – provided the journalistic melodrama, Jeffrey delivered vintage Augustan sentiment to British readers, the maintenance of whose collective self-image – the battered elite – entailed their reading their favourite weeklies as a sort of self-medication whilst their country and culture went to the dogs.

The intensely negative criticism that buried Keats's reputation at the time would keep it low until long after his death. Few critics who prided themselves on not needing their Greek translated for them could admire Keats's work without reservations. They knew that when they themselves had learned the language at university, their chief difficulty consisted in gaining an understanding of every idea which it expressed, even though it used words for which there were no precise matches in English. In learning Greek in a systematic way at university, the future reviewer had

had to identify in his mind the margins of new realms of ideas, with the result that realms of ideas would grow where none had been earlier. In this way, he not only learned words, but he gained ideas too: somewhat other expressions than are used in the original language need to be used by the translator. The concept to be translated has to be broken up and reorganised. This is the very activity that can train and upgrade the growing mind out of *youth* (the ancient Greek for which was *uneducated*) and into the eminence of the man of letters – from the shine of an alpha-arbitrator like Croker to the finish of a 'Z' like Lockhart. For such time-served intellectuals, it must have seemed routine enough to take it that Keats's ideas, inspired by and expressed in his native language rather than in the language of Homer, underwent no higher modifications or deeper shadings between conception and execution. For Keats's key critics, he simply had not had the direct means of mental culture that could have corrected and matured his ideas by giving prominence to their many-sided natures and their different ranges of connotations. All he seemed to his critics to be able to do was salivate sublimely over the most lip-smacking use of the English language. 'There is a cool pleasure,' he wrote as a marginal note on *Paradise Lost* (I, 321), 'in the very sound of the word vale. The English word is of the happiest chance … It is a sort of Delphic Abstraction – a beautiful thing made more beautiful by being reflected and put in a mist.' This may suggest a lexical imagination, but when one thinks of Keats's 'Vale of Soul-making' (*Letters*, I, p.102), and his determination to suffer profitably, one feels that his vision has been hard-won, and not just superficially written about.

Keats had read in Gilbert Burnet's *History of My Own Times* that *Paradise Lost* was 'the beautifullest and perfectest poem that ever was writ'. But (felt some key critics) in the process of learning the real language of Homer, Keats's ideas could have become more independent of words, with the result of his paying keener attention to the weight and worth of words, and their assembly and organisation. He could have learned how to make them fixed and fluid with superior accuracy, and so he could have become more properly skilled, not only at expressing essential thoughts, but at preserving them as well. Furthermore, he could have learned to feel the right level of respect for the English language, and thus have been protected from any attempt to adapt it in such an irresponsible and uninformed way. (He would then, surely, not have had the temerity to declare that he 'look[ed] upon fine Phrases like a Lover.') There was the general feeling in the literary establishment of Keats's time that if even one classically uneducated writer could publish and remain unscathed, the profession of author would be brought into justifiable disrepute.

And yet, even as all the hostility had come to a head, Keats himself is said by some to have remained contemplative and sublime – even shamanic – in his indifference to ideas about him in the heads of others: 'Praise or blame has but a momentary effect on the man whose love of beauty in the abstract makes him a severe critic on his own Works. My own domestic criticism has given me pain without comparison beyond what Blackwood or the Quarterly could possibly inflict. [A]nd also when I feel I am right, no external praise can give me such a glow as my own solitary reperception & ratification of what is fine … [*Endymion*] is as good as I had power to make it – by myself'. Keats's passionate ownership of his latest product, despite its being despised so emphatically by the critics, has something of Goethe's maxim: 'Whatever you can do, or dream you can, begin it. Boldness has genuine power and magic in it.' Keats: 'Had I been nervous about its being a perfect piece, & with that view asked advice, & trembled over every page, it would not have been written; for it is not in my nature to fumble – I will write independently.'

Five years after the poet's death, in January 1826, readers of *Blackwood's Magazine* were still being kept 'right' (in more than one sense) with regard to Keats: 'He outhunted Hunt in a species of emasculated pruriency, that … looks as if it were the product of some imaginative Eunuch's muse within the melancholy inspiration of the Haram.' In 1845, De Quincey (an outstanding Greek scholar, and proud of it) complained about Keats's failure to tread carefully on the 'holy … *language* of his country'. De Quincey bemoaned Keats's having 'trampled as with the hoofs of a buffalo' where other writers (such as, of course, De Quincey himself) could receive and adapt ancient knowledge with more happily inherited instincts of authority, economy and grace.

Keats's 'limitations' and 'want of tact' were not the only things about him to excite negative or begrudging comments. He was assumed by some commentators to lack character. Even Hazlitt, notable for his fondness for Keats, said in 1824 (three years after the poet's death) that 'All [Keats] wanted was manly strength and fortitude.' The sentiment is worth thinking about: how one thinks about it can determine how highly one values Keats's achievement. The man who prides himself on having, or admiring exclusively, character – the sort of moral-fibre that wins (or at least fights just) wars, implements (or at least formulates with good intentions) systems of thought, gets (or at least tries for) job promotions, and beats (or at least bravely fights) diseases – is not very likely to have the following as his adage: 'I have clung/To nothing, lov'd a nothing,

nothing seen/Or felt but a great dream!' (IV, 636-8) This is actually Endymion's expression of self-reproach as he leaves the Cave of Quietude in the realisation that the things for which he wishes are beyond the ken of ordinary men: 'O I have been/Presumptuous against love, against the sky,/Against all elements, against the tie/Of mortals each to each.' (IV, 638-41) Keats's 'lack' was supposed to go hand in hand with his 'sugary' style of poetry. The Scottish historian and political philosopher Thomas Carlyle (1795-1881), who in *Sartor Resartus* (1840) paid honour to the 'strong, just man' as against the apathetic, corrupted masses, said that 'Keats wanted a world of treacle!' While Victorian readers (including a great many women) did take pleasure in Keats's poems as exquisite – but, importantly, temporary – flights from their hemmed-in and humdrum lives, the Victorian readership in the (male) main preferred more ostentatiously backboned poets (which was why Wordsworth's popularity increased as it did during his later years, and still more after his death in 1850). Matthew Arnold expressed disappointment with Keats after reading Monckton Milnes's biography of the poet in 1848: 'What harm he has done in English Poetry. As Browning is a man with a moderate gift passionately desiring movement and fullness, and obtaining but a confused multitudinousness, so Keats with a very high gift, is yet also consumed by this desire: and cannot produce the truly living and moving, as his conscience keeps telling him.' (*The Letters of Mathew Arnold to Arthur Hugh Clough* [edited by Howard Foster Lowry], 1932, p.97) And in a letter to Sidney Colvin in June 1887, Arnold's recognition of what is good about *Endymion* is, if anything, discreet, whereas his grieving over the expanse of waste from which he feels condemned to pick what is worthwhile is more plainly in view: 'What is good in *Endymion* is not, to my mind, so good as you say, and the poem as a whole I could wish to have been suppressed and lost. I really resent the space it occupies in the volumes of Keats's poetry.'

Later, the twentieth-century critics tended to agree that Keats's promise was greater than his achievement. There seems to be – as Arnold made clear above – something voluminously, nay monumentally, self-debunking about *Endymion*. The sheer quantity of the poem seems to have obliged even admirers of the poet's more achieved 'fits and starts' (such as the great odes) to include the whole shebang, and they have included every extant block in their evaluation of the poet's overall achievement, instead of delighting – no less learnedly – in the quintessence he left behind. In *The Use of Poetry and the Use of Criticism* (1933), T.S. Eliot (1888-1965) said that Keats's views on poetry as expressed in his letters show that his critical acuity was superior to the poetry he wrote. Faint praise indeed from one poet to another. Eliot was not the only influential figure to advise modern readers not to waste too much time with Keats's poetry. William Empson (1906-84), F.R. Leavis (1895-1978), I.A. Richards (1893-1979) and the other entrepreneurs of social realism were all busy razing everything to the discursive level – a level at which, say, Keats's belief in 'nothing but of the holiness of the Heart's affections and the truth of Imagination' (*Letters*, I, p.184) would look like a crank's proclamation without a trace of seriousness to interest the modern passer-by; something to be tidied away in the box of 'outgrown' modes of thought and discourse marked 'Romantic'.

4

'Isabella; or, the Pot of Basil'

Arnold would express disappointment with the overall effect of Keats's 'Isabella; or, the Pot of Basil', despite its isolated aesthetic assets:

> The poem of Isabella, then, is a perfect treasure-house of graceful and felicitous words and images: almost in every stanza there occurs one of those vivid and picturesque turns of expression, by which the object is made to flash upon the eye of the mind, and which thrill the reader with a sudden delight. [Arnold's little tribute to Wordsworth's 'inward eye' and daffodils suggests the expectations underpinning his critical approach.] This one short poem contains, perhaps, a greater number of happy single expressions which one could quote than all the extant tragedies of Sophocles. But the action, the story? The action itself is an excellent one; but so feebly is it conceived by the Poet, so loosely constructed, that the effect produced by it, in and for itself, is absolutely null. (*Keats: Narrative Poems*, p.54)

The judgment, be it remembered of the Professor of Poetry at Oxford (1857-62), would be inwardly digested on a widespread basis.

Keats did not want this poem, based on a story by Giovanni Boccaccio (1313-75), to be published. In her essay, 'The Material Sublime: Keats and *Isabella*' (1974), Louise Z. Smith (not to be confused with the other 'Z') has resisted the general negativity about 'Isabella; or, the Pot of Basil', but she has still felt the need to call the poem 'the wallflower among Keats's narratives.' (*Keats: Narrative Poems*, p.105) Richard Woodhouse would tell John Taylor that Keats 'could not bear ["Isabella"] now [some 18 months after writing it]. It appeared to him mawkish.' (*Letters*, II, p.162) Keats himself would write to Woodhouse:

<blockquote>
I will give you a few reasons why I shall persist in not publishing The Pot of Basil – It is too smokeable – I can get it smoak'd at the Carpenters shaving chimney much more cheaply – There is too much inexperience of live, and simplicity of knowledge in it – which might do very well after one's death – but not while one is alive. There are very few would look to the reality. I intend to use more finesse with the Public. It is possible to write fine things which cannot be laugh'd at in any way. Isabella is what I should call were I a reviewer 'A weak-sided Poem' with an amusing sober-sadness about it. (Letters, II, p.174)
</blockquote>

Keats was worried that wits about town reviewing 'Isabella' might recognise his lack of experience – and, in particular, his lack of sexual experience – and scribble with amusement at his expense (or smoke him, as Keats, borrowing the term from Restoration comedy, put it). He was right to worry, given that (to give just one instance) he had referred to Isabella's breasts in the poem as 'Those dainties made to still an infant's cries'.

Keats's poem does convey his distaste for the real world of commerce: ' … many a weary hand did swelt/In torched mines and noisy factories … ' (XIV). At the beginning of the poem, the humble Lorenzo's two deceitful and ruthless employers do not know that their sister, Isabella, is Lorenzo's lover. The brothers' plan has always been 'to coax her by degrees/To some high noble and his olive trees.' (XXI) When the treacherous brothers – 'these money-bags', or 'ledger-men' – find out that Isabella and Lorenzo have been secretly attached, they plan to murder Lorenzo:

> And many a jealous conference had they,
> And many times they bit their lips alone,
> Before they fix'd upon the surest way
> To make the youngster for his crime atone;
> And at the last, these men of cruel clay
> Cut Mercy with a sharp knife to the bone;
> For they resolved in some forest dim
> To kill Lorenzo, and there bury him. (XXII)

One can see the young poet's continuing struggle to work his various resources into a credible unity. (Can 'Mercy' in any convincing sense be 'Cut … with a sharp knife to the bone'?) A little later, Keats allows the reader to witness Lorenzo being led 'Into a forest quiet for the slaughter', but the poet decides to leave it – for the time being – to the reader's imagination exactly how the slaughter happens, saying only: 'There was Lorenzo slain and buried in,/There in that forest did his great love cease … ' (XXVIII). Just as some of Wordsworth's best narrative verses can follow with empathy the feelings of a woman abandoned by an unscrupulous man and left destitute with her child (as in 'The Mad Mother'), so Keats documents Isabella's psychological deterioration since hearing of the loss of her lover:

> They told their sister how, with sudden speed,
> Lorenzo had ta'en ship for foreign lands,
> Because of some great urgency and need
> In their affairs requiring trusty hands.
> Poor Girl! Put on thy stifling widow's weed,
> And 'scape at once from Hope's accursed bands;
> To-day thou wilt not see him, nor to-morrow,
> And the next day will be a day of sorrow.
>
> She weeps alone for pleasures not to be;
> Sorely she wept until the night came on,
> And then, instead of love, O Misery!
> She brooded o'er the luxury alone:
> His image in the dusk she seem'd to see,
> And to the silence made a gentle moan,
> Spreading her perfect arms upon the air,
> And on her couch low murmuring 'Where? O where?' (XXIX-XXX)

When one compares these verses to Keats's later works (such as 'The Eve of St Agnes' or the great odes), it is hard to disagree with the view that he (writing 'Isabella' in March and April 1818) had not reached his full maturity.

Claude L. Finney's *Evolution of Keats* (1936) and Bernard Blackstone's *The Consecrated Urn: An Interpretation of Keats in Terms of Growth and Form* (1959) both place 'Isabella' in the context of Keats's peculiarly rapid progress as a poet. The poem's progression of tableaux is, arguably, not informed by the sort of persuasively consistent principles behind, say, Wordsworth's narrative poetry. Still experimenting with different tones and techniques, Keats can show his Wordsworthian understanding of the unhappy Isabella in one stanza, and then generate the Gothic phosphorescence of her vision (in which she learns the true circumstances surrounding her lover's disappearance) in the next:

> [Dead Lorenzo's] eyes, though wild, were still all dewy bright
> With love, and kept all phantom fear aloof
> From the poor girl by magic of their light,
> The while it did unthread the horrid woof
> Of the late darken'd time, – the murderous spite
> Of pride and avarice, – the dark pine roof
> In the forest, – and the sodden turfed dell,
> Where, without any word, from stabs he fell. (XXXVII)

The reader learns about the manner of Lorenzo's death only now, with Isabella, and through the ghostly messenger, 'the pale shadow' (XXXVI). Hence Keats, not yet able to work over the raw materials of a story with comprehensive mastery, still feels some pressure to wave, as it were, a wand of the Gothic kind.

The indistinctness of narrative tone remains troubling throughout the poem. The way Lorenzo's head looks when Isabella disinters his body is problematic: 'Ah! wherefore all this wormy circumstance?/Why linger at the yawning tomb so long?' (XLIX) Is the faint resonance of Cyril Tourneur's (1570-1626) 'bony lady' (*The Revenger's Tragedy*, Act III, scene v, 119) intentional? Or is the narrative meant to be a little Byronic (that is, ebullient and lightly blasphemous) at this point? (Keats did admire Byron very much: he had dressed like him at school, and he had written the admiring sonnet, 'Byron! how sweetly sad thy melody!', in 1814.) Perhaps his real boldness (or ineptitude) is in the way he retains the element of compassion for Isabella, even as she, helped by 'that aged Dame' (XLIV), severs Lorenzo's head from the rest of his body:

> In anxious secrecy they took it home,
> And then the prize was all for Isabel:
> She calm'd its wild hair with a golden comb,
> And all around each eye's sepulchral cell
> Pointed each fringed lash; the smeared loam
> With tears, as chilly as a dripping well,
> She drench'd away: – and still she comb'd, and kept
> Sighing all day – and still she kiss'd, and wept. (LI)

For John Whale, no wonder Keats – whose poetic sophistication would continue to increase exponentially – became more anxious about the poem's reception:

Faced with such pathological detail [as in the stanza above] many readers will immediately consign this part of the poem to the category ludicrous. There's something deeply unsettling about Isabella's activity here, and not simply because it strains the credibility of a forensically informed imagination. It is, for one thing, horribly reminiscent of a girl's grooming of her doll, right down to the straightening of the eye-lashes. (*Critical Issues: John Keats*, p.63)

Now in his twenties, and nearing his full potential, but with the lingering adolescence still to be burnt off as he continued to transform himself, Keats would often find himself embarrassed by last year's – or even last month's – effort. It could be suggested, however, that Whale's appreciation of the poem has been reductively forensic (and even misleadingly finicky) when it could have been more expansive, or, to use Spenser's epithet (that Keats adored) for a whale at one with its environment, 'sea-shouldering'. In Boccaccio's *Decameron*, Lorenzo's body had been untouched by decay and putrefaction – it was the apprentice surgeon Keats who introduced a perishable Lorenzo. Keats's Isabella will eventually be left with no material Lorenzo – just a lover's memories and intense grief (not actually there, materially, to be measured by her money-bags brothers, but real all the same).

The exhumation of Lorenzo is Isabella's soul's desperate attempt to connect again with her cruelly dispatched lover. Keats knows that expressions of soul are misrepresented in this world. And the soul is too often reduced to feeding on what it does not really hunger for. The brothers misrepresented Lorenzo and deprived Isabella of that which she most needed (namely, the love of Lorenzo), but she – in touch with her own soul – got to know better. Whale seems to imagine in Keats's Isabella the essential inhumanity of (Whale's idea of) a child with a doll (like a serial killer with a corpse). But Keats's psychological acuity is like Shakespeare's in that it can make an old story newly haunting, and it completely outsoars crime scene investigations. Does Hamlet's fascination with the late Yorick's skull consign the graveside scene in *Hamlet* to 'the category ludicrous'? The dead human head, like the ruins of Tintern Abbey, may be touched by presences for which there is no empirical evidence – all we have is the impression of Hamlet's fondness for Yorick who had carried him on his back a thousand times, and who had set the table on a roar with his flashes of merriment. All we have is Isabella's obvious and inextinguishable love for her chop-falling (remember, not yet chop-fallen) Lorenzo. How abhorred in the imagination it is. One's gorge rises at it. One's need for further support in open court is self-evidently superfluous.

The whole issue may be revisited helpfully in the context of Benjamin Bailey's recollection of Keats's own (living) head:

> [Keats] bore, along with the strong impress of genius, much beauty of feature & countenance ... His hair was beautiful – a fine brown, rather than auburn, I think; & if you placed your hand upon his head, the silken curls felt like the rich plumage of a bird. I do not particularly remember the thickness of the upper lip, which is so generally described, & doubtless correctly; – but the mouth struck me as too wide, both in itself, & as out of harmony with the rest of the face, which, with this single blemish, was eminently beautiful. The eye was full & fine, & softened into tenderness, or beamed with a fiery brightness, according to the current of his thoughts and conversation. Indeed the form of his head was like that of a fine Greek statue: – & he realised to my mind the youthful Apollo, more than any head of a living man whom I have known.

The spirit of genius that animates Keats's living head is large. The spirit of love for Isabella that animated Lorenzo's head before he was murdered would have been what the poor woman desperately desired to recapture. And who knows what Whale might have written if the thought of Gherardi's death-mask of Keats, taken on 24 February 1821, the day after Keats died, had swum into his ken?

Today, as in Keats's time, two-dimensional critics sit in judgement of three-dimensional poetry. (There are exceptions: at least, for example, the creators of the Reduced Shakespeare Company have seen the joke!) For some reason, a rank and file academic's comprehension of the words of a great poet is supposed to settle the matter as far as such a 'matter' can be 'settled'. That is, 'objective' *comp*rehension is routinely supposed, at schools' and universities' English departments, to be more useful than an intimate *app*rehension of the great poet's enriching and expansive presence. 'An extensive knowledge is needful to thinking people,' Keats told John Hamilton Reynolds (1794-1852), ' – it takes away the heat and fever; and helps, by widening speculation, to ease the Burden of the Mystery'. Keats did not know that, hundreds of years hence, young examinees would be responding to the sensuous imagery in his Odes –

to say nothing of the irony of Jane Austen, or the originality of the *Lyrical Ballads* – in order to demonstrate transferrable skills in accordance with governmentally-formulated assessment-objectives. So many young persons' approaches to Keats must necessarily be disingenuous, because so many are expected to cotton on to what is 'more' important: parroting from behind the disguise of classroom decorum is more likely to get you somewhere (a decent-paying job, a house, a car, safe company for the children, and so on) than wasting your finer feelings. As Moses John Jackson says in Tom Stoppard's play, *The Invention of Love* (1997), 'I've got nothing against poetry, don't think I have, I like a good poem as well as the next man, but … '.

In July 1820, Charles Lamb had the geniality and generosity to pick out the beauties of 'Isabella' rather than linger over the poem's deficiencies:

> Two Florentines, merchants, discovering that their sister Isabella has placed her affections upon Lorenzo, a young factor in their employ, when they had hopes of procuring for her a noble match, decoy Lorenzo, under pretence of a ride, into a wood, where they suddenly stab and bury him. The anticipation of the assassination is wonderfully conceived in one epithet, in the narration of the ride –
>
> So the two brothers, and their *murder'd* man,
> Rode past fair Florence, to where Arno's stream
> Gurgles – (*Keats: Narrative Poems*, p.52).

A reviewer in the *New Monthly Magazine* acclaimed the poem's 'naked and affecting simplicity which goes straight to the heart', but the reviewer added that the poem had 'no[t] the rich love-scenes of Barry Cornwall's *A Sicilian Story*' (*Critical Issues: John Keats*, p.56). The sense of the young poet still aspiring to better, but in the meantime still having to crank out what he can, is difficult to ignore, and even poignant:

> Then in a silken scarf, – sweet with the dews
> Of precious flowers pluck'd in Araby,
> And divine liquids come with odorous ooze
> Through the cold serpent-pipe refreshfully, –
> She wrapp'd it up; and for its tomb did choose
> A garden-pot, wherein she laid it by,
> And cover'd it with mould, and o'er it set
> Sweet Basil, which her tears kept ever wet. (LII)

For Louise Smith, 'Isabella' is Keats's 'last poetic failure'. In writing it, it is as if Keats was self-administering homeopathic allusions to Greek myth, continuing to set himself up for higher and higher poetic pollen counts:

> Moan hither, all ye syllables of woe,
> From the deep throat of sad Melpomene!
> Through bronzed lyre in tragic order go,
> And touch the strings into a mystery;
> Sound mournfully upon the winds and low;
> For simple Isabel is soon to be
> Among the dead: She withers, like a palm
> Cut by an Indian for its juicy balm. (LVI)

'Moan hither … ' cannot be taken seriously by the post- (and does not appear to have impressed the pre-) modern reader. Keats anticipated contemporary reviewers' reactions to the poem: 'it … might do very well after one's death – but not while one is alive. There are very few would look to the reality.' (*Letters*, II, p.174) Arnold would be singeing in his opinion of how the poem compared with the work it purported to emulate: 'Let the reader, after he has finished the poem … turn to the same story in the Decameron [of Boccaccio]: he will then feel how pregnant and interesting the same action has become in the hands of a great artist, who above all things delineates his object; who subordinates expression to that which it is designed to express … ' (*Keats: Narrative Poems*, p.54).

Anyhow, the young poet completes the story. The brothers 'watch'd in vain;/For seldom did she go to chapel-shrift,/And seldom felt she any hunger-pain … ' (LIX). Curious as to the reason for Isabella's self-neglect, they steal the basil-pot, and find that 'The thing was vile with green and livid spot,/And yet they knew it was Lorenzo's face … ' (LX). They flee in guilty horror, but not before taking the basil pot from their sister. Isabella is left with nothing, and has nothing to look forward to: 'And so she pined, and so she died forlorn' (LXIII). Now, at the age of 23, Keats himself had less than three years left to live, but he was becoming sublimely attuned to the most important (least material) exigencies of existence, and the 'innumerable compositions and decompositions which take place between the intellect and its thousand materials before it arrives at that trembling delicate and snail-horn perception of Beauty.'

5

'On Sitting Down to Read *King Lear* Once Again'

Writing this poem in January 1818 (before 'Isabella'), Keats signals a marked intensification of the poet's golden raptness that initially took hold of him on first looking into Chapman's Homer. He tells 'Golden tongued Romance' to take her 'serene lute' away because the sound, however lovely, does not really represent the actual struggles of life. So why invoke her in the first place?

> O Golden tongued Romance, with serene lute!
>   Fair plumed Syren, Queen of far-away!
>   Leave melodizing on this wintry day,
> Shut up thine olden pages, and be mute:
> Adieu!

This formal dismissal of a key part of one's being has something of the drama of George Herbert's (1593-1633) spiritual discontent – and his momentary desire to tear himself away from it – at the beginning of 'The Collar':

> I struck the board, and cry'd, No more.
>   I will abroad.
>   What? shall I ever sigh and pine?
> My lines and life are free; free as the rode,
>   Loose as the winde, as large as store.

Many individuals try to achieve independence, or at least the feeling of independence, by some sort of declaration (followed by some decisive behaviour, or even some emotional violence, to make good that declaration). One is tempted continually to lock oneself up within a new system in order to live there in some sort of peace with the world and oneself. Such a peace, however, would only be temporary, and would grant one merely a different kind of damnation which would compel one to renege perpetually. To remain independent it would always be necessary to be devising a new structure, and the exertion entailed would be an exacting penalty. By the end of 'The Collar', having vented some of the pent up frustration of his unrewarded piety, Herbert will again be ready to return to his 'board' and his God. By the end of *King Lear*, having sloughed off his burdensome kingship, and having then felt how sharper than serpents' teeth people will be when no longer officially obliged to respect him, Lear will see again the love he has always shared with Cordelia. Shakespeare knows that Lear's scheme for a new system to cushion him in his dotage is like any human being's rejection of his own soul and all its tiresome baggage. At the time the gesture of rejecting can feel liberating and lightening, but it will lead to misery and madness, because spontaneous, unexpected upshots of life's general vitality – or indeed its relentless entropy – will spill and swell, sooner or later, with a force ruinous to even the most fiercely turreted resolutions. Anyone who has struggled to keep a New Year's resolution knows how fluently temptation can speak the language of rectitude, and with what puritanical airs wantonness will subvert the best intentions. If one attempts to move or extend any of the values informing one's current entrenchment, one will always straggle behind the uncontrollable energy of life, and yet one will never really want to stop pursuing multiform, multicoloured, mysterious beauty as it moves outside one's limits on its own limitless terms. Cordelia's death was so shocking to Dr Johnson that he could not bear to reread *King Lear* for years. But what Shakespeare had taught could not be unlearned, regardless of how long it took any reader, Johnson included, to steel himself for another wintry blast of the essential truth that is unwelcome in the false paradise of most literary culture.

Sentenced interminably to the mortification of a new transition, one might take a radically different decision: to avoid the unpleasantness of philosophical apostasies, one might proudly resign oneself to diffidence, and become more at ease with dreaming, and feeling, rather than attempting again in vain to think things through thoroughly – that is, one might look for sanctuary in unimpeachable naivety. S.T. Coleridge's troubled son, Hartley, formulated this state of simplicity in some of his poetry:

> I would not have the restless will
> That hurries to and fro
> Searching for some great things to do
> Or secret thing to know
> I would be treated as a child
> And guided where to go.

This is where many people think they would settle and put their scruples to rest. But they cannot. People tend to know only too well that at least two thirds of their progeny, other relatives, or friends will be capable of behaving badly towards them. And people tend to know – as William Blake (1757-1827) did when he wrote 'Jerusalem' – that if one does not have one's own system, one will be enslaved by someone else's. Even a so-called Fool can tell a king why a snail has a house: 'Why, to put's head in; not to give it away to his daughters, and leave his horns without a case.' (*King Lear*, Act I, scene 5, 26) Ignorance, or feigned ignorance, of what Keats called 'the agonies, the strife/Of human hearts' (*Sleep and Poetry*, 124-5) will not save you from your own agonies, and the fierily restless mind (and whatever it is that burns beneath that), as Byron knows, will not be 'snuffed out'. By rereading *King Lear*, and thence involving himself in the 'fierce dispute/Betwixt damnation and impassion'd clay', Keats is being, in a sense, ceremonial, and offering himself up to the 'Begetters of our deep eternal theme'. Strangely, he is taking a break from revising his problematically Romantic *Endymion* when he is interrupted, so to speak, by an urgent messenger (the author of *King Lear*) arrived out of the dark, and he is possessed thereafter by a fresh energy already beginning to make him think and write differently. The delivery from the dark includes Lear's horrible words: 'my poor fool is hanged!' (Act V, scene 3, 305) The inescapable meaning of these words is that it is Cordelia, not the 'Fool', who has been hanged. Why does Shakespeare have Lear refer to his most loving, but now tragically dead, daughter as a fool? It may be something to do with the dementia, or lexical loosening, as one slips into the dark (Lear dies just 16 lines later). Or, as Edgar puts it almost at the very end of the play, 'The weight of this sad time we must obey;/Speak what we feel, not what we ought to say.' (Act V, scene 3, 323-4)

Keats feels that in too much of *Endymion* he has been saying what he thought he ought to say. He himself, at his worst, has been speaking from behind his (not always convincing) mask of poetic decorum. *King Lear* teaches him that he cannot really escape the most terrible energies of life simply by dilating the sphere of Romance and disappearing into it. Lear's request to his imaginary apothecary for civet to sweeten his state of mind (Act IV, scene 6, 129) is made by a desperate man on the run from bitter clarity. In his earlier poem, 'Fill for me the Brimming Bowl', Keats had already begun to shine some light on what he himself was running from, but he was still (like most people) habitually tempted to relieve himself of the pressures of present anxieties by redoubling his commitment to ad hoc asceticism. He well knew that the approach was not relevant enough to the complexity of the challenges, and he knew that it would simply, and therefore only temporarily, seem to shield him against life's thousand shocks. The ache for female company, for example, was to Keats, in certain moods, such a distressingly enslaving sensation that it brought about in him the equally tumescent urge to rid himself of it entirely, perhaps as Odysseus had himself tied to his ship's mast in order to stop himself from abandoning the ship in pursuit of the sirens at the sound of their ravishing voices:

> Fill for me the brimming bowl
> And let me in it drown my soul:
> But put therein some drug, designed
> To Banish Women from my mind:
> For I want not the stream inspiring
> That fills the mind with – fond desiring,
> But I want as deep a draught
> As e'er from Lethe's wave was quaff'd …

In one mood, having impetuously wanted to burn off the sexual impulse once and for all, there is now, in another mood, a part of Keats that wants to burn *Endymion*. He wants rid of it because he recognises it as something that he really should have left behind long ago if he is to become the sort of poet he most wants to be. But as Motion points out, 'He had invested too much in it, too publicly, and he had been advanced money he could not afford to return. He gritted his teeth and pressed on … ' (Motion, p.223). One of the strengths of Motion's biography is in its continual alertness to the material circumstances that were always grinding Keats through the mill.

The writing of *Endymion* brought Keats to a fascinating point in his poetic development, like the draughty and uncomfortable predicament of a new life half in and half out of the womb. Or, to put it another way, he was inspirited by new hopes, yet he was still situated amidst the smouldering ruins of his former hopes. His desire for purification and transcendence was violent. On being touched by the sparks from *King Lear*, Keats knew what must become of his own build-up of brushwood around him – and he longed to be 'cooked', or transmuted, in the very flames raised so magically by a pre-Enlightenment bard (and shirked so instinctively by an 'Enlightened' lexicographer). If it was through Chapman that the first glow of lasting consequence got into Keats's work, it was through Shakespeare that the powerful refining flame with which he would ultimately transform himself was now issuing.

6

'When I Have Fears that I May Cease to Be'

Written in January 1818, the same month as the Lear sonnet, 'When I Have Fears' provides more evidence of Keats's resolve to cleave to, at the risk of having his wings singed by, the lambencies of Shakespeare's cadences –

> When I do count the clock that tells the time,
> And see the brave day sunk in hideous night;
> When I behold the violet past prime,
> And sable curls all silvered o'er with white (Shakespeare, Sonnet 12) –

which, as already seen (in *King Lear*), can flare into harder flames around a harder theme, and most particularly in the rarer mind of an open reader. But, after what Keats himself called the 'ranting' of 'On Sitting Down to Read King Lear Once Again', 'When I have fears' throws a calmer focus of the poet's lynx beam down through the lower levels of the troubled mind, right through the region where fears and fancies flourish, to a region (half in the dreaming, half in the waking, mind) in which problems are frozen into 'naked and grecian' clarity. The deeper truth is, as Shakespeare said in *A Midsummer Night's Dream*, something of great constancy – and Keats is again trembling on the point of psychic discovery before bringing out of himself a product of mind with the permanent urgency that remains in place despite receding in time, even after the artist himself has melted (as poor Yorick and Lorenzo had) back into the universal flux. His admiration of Shakespeare, as expressed in letters to friends, effects the prose backdrop to Keats's poetry at this time: for Keats, Shakespeare 'was just like any other man, but … he was like all other men. He was the least of an egoist that it was possible to be. He was nothing in himself; but he was all that others were, or that they could become. He not only had in himself the germs of every faculty and feeling, but he could follow them by anticipation, intuitively, into all their conceivable ramifications, through every change of fortune, or conflict of passion, or turn of thought … When he conceived of a character, whether real or imaginary, he not only entered into all its thoughts and feelings, but seemed instantly, and as if by touching a secret spring, to be surrounded with all the same objects.' It was with something of the shaman's gift that Shakespeare spirited himself behind Cordelia's eyes, and it was with a similar gift that Keats spirited himself behind Isabella's.

Keats's fears that he might 'cease to be' may bring to the mind the apprehension of death that has led countless individuals to total despair. One of the most highly polished expressions of the collective shock can now be found in Larkin's 'Aubade', in which it is a given (rather than a fear) that each of us will 'cease to be' because on pronouncement of death we will have 'no sight, no sound,/No touch or taste or smell, nothing to think with,/Nothing to love or link with'. However, Keats's idea of ceasing to be is the richer for its lack of the twentieth century's almost absolute commitment to its own self-annihilating procedures. (Keats is more interested in leaving behind great thoughts shining in imperishable poetry than he is in reminding the reader to gown up for any 'anaesthetic from which none come round.') Keats has something of Prospero's visions in *The Tempest* which, though made from a 'fabric' beyond any sight, sound, touch, taste or smell ('baseless'), are clearly not just symptoms of any God delusion. Keats's sun is maturing, and his life is getting autumnal. His brain is fruitful, misty and 'teeming', and there is an abundance to be 'glean'd' before the winter sets in.

7

'To Homer'

Written in April or May 1818, this poem celebrates the vision of the author of the *Odyssey*, about whom almost nothing is known. It is thought that Homer was born on the island of Chios and was blind. It has even been suggested that he was actually a woman. Deprived of the facts, the scholar or translator of Homer will be forced back upon intuition and speculation. In other words, however trained to handle, say, tenses, adjectives and adverbs, the individual with no taste for poetry will be ill-equipped to receive the poetry. A poet's antennae and special powers of orientation are prerequisites. 'Standing aloof in giant ignorance', Keats's Homer is simultaneously a colossal icon and a humanly unknowing intelligence, and this suggests, without force, the soul that sees, transcends, and shows other souls the way. In this mode of wisdom and communication, imagination effortlessly shines through, and as it does this, the whole network of the unimaginative world is sightless, and powerless, by comparison. Keats's Homer is one of the towering beacon-fires (or perhaps even a tower transmitting radio signals) recognised and relied upon with such gratitude by mariners of the mind's ocean.

It is useful to compare Keats's Homer to another's. In the twentieth century, T.E. Lawrence (1888-1935) would say that Homer's 'pages are steeped in a queer naivety; and at our remove of thought and language we cannot guess if he is smiling or not.' Lawrence goes on to say something about Homer that could have a smack of Keats: 'Yet there is a dignity which compels respect and baffles us … '. However, unlike Lawrence, Keats will not just tolerate his own bafflement – he will even preserve its purity as the best means of tuning in to higher truth, like Orpheus tuning his lyre or the Sufi polishing his mirror. One can sense Lawrence's irritable reaching out for the facts and the reasons that will solve his Homer puzzle: 'In four years of living with [*The Odyssey*] I have tried to deduce the author from his self-betrayal in the work. I found a book-worm, no longer young, living from home, a mainlander, city-bred and domestic. Married but not exclusively, a dog-lover, often hungry and thirsty, dark-haired.' Sir Arthur Conan Doyle (1859-1930) himself could not have sounded more like Sherlock Holmes sifting through circumstantial evidence, and talking like a sort of droll telegram from the other side of time. This is the kind of verbiage in which intellectuals to this day have discovered that they can self-preen without seeming to. Meanwhile, the 'deep seas' teem untouched by them, and the presences of the 'dolphin-coral' remain unvisited by them.

Given that Homer lived in the pre-archaeological eighth century BC, Lawrence's Holmes-inspired approach is merely pent up within the limits of contemporary life and culture. Lawrence says that Homer was 'Fond of poetry' and that he had a 'limited sensuous range but an exact eyesight which gave him all his pictures.' Lawrence's Homer was also a 'lover of old bric-a-brac, though as muddled an antiquary as Walter Scott … '. So goes the flat and clever voice of a familiarly intellectual type of ego: as it provides the running commentary on its own search for the contradictions that will eliminate, say, one unnecessary line of enquiry here, and perhaps another there, it generates more (and much less necessary) contradictions, and litter-loutishly leaves the results like some niggling regatta on the ocean of truth, in plain view of the shore. And so the next generation of thinkers, instinctively glancing for directions as they ease themselves down the shelves for the first time, see the litter, but they fail to recognise it as litter until they have been misled by it – until they too have spent their best years unconnectedly buoyant. Since the European Enlightenment, intellectuals have seemed to continue – despite the Romantics' most eloquent protestations – to articulate and problematize many issues of human interest beyond the brink of human interest.

With lines such as 'There is a budding morrow in midnight,/There is a triple sight in blindness keen', 'To Homer' shows Keats as something like Coleridge's speculative depiction of a 'great Poet', who

> must be, implicitè if not explicitè, a profound Metaphysician. He may not have [any metaphysical idea] in logical coherence, in his Brain & Tongue; but he must have it by *Tact*/for all sounds, & all forms of human nature he must have the *ear* of a wild Arab listening in the silent Desart, the eye of a North American Indian tracing the footsteps of an Enemy upon the Leaves that strew the Forest – ; the *Touch* of a Blind Man feeling the face of a darling Child. (Coleridge to Sotheby, 1802)

For Keats, the poet can, 'with a bird,/Wren or Eagle, find … his way to/All its instincts'. For Keats, all experience 'Comes articulate and presseth/On his ear like mother-tongue'. ('The Poet') Keats is standing, like Homer, aloof in giant ignorance. He has an empathy with Homer (who felt his own soul, and its exchanging and receiving) as he had an empathy with Isabella (who felt hers). If Keats is 'ignorant' (of high culture, as his harshest critics say), and Homer 'was … blind', and Isabella was kept in the dark by her brothers about Lorenzo's whereabouts, 'the veil' could still be 'rent', the truth could still be 'uncurtain'd', and depths of being could be revealed to surface consciousness: 'Such seeing hadst thou, as it once befell/To Dian, Queen of Earth, and Heaven, and Hell.' Only with poetry can we lift ourselves – however briefly – out of excessive intellectualism's deepening litter.

8

Hyperion

Written mostly between September and December 1818, in blank verse (which had freed Milton from 'the bondage of rhyming'), *Hyperion* represents the filling out of Keats's potential into the substantiality of great achievement. Making good his earlier claim of independence from the classically trained critics, Keats again found his theme in Greek mythology. Saturn is introduced as a 'fallen divinity' (I, 12) like Milton's Lucifer, damaged and darkened by his fall, and contagious – 'Spreading a shade' (I, 13). When one reads these opening lines, one could be looking at a great painting, in which the usual traffic of the elements has been silenced – 'No stir of air' (I, 7), 'A stream went voiceless by, still deadened more' (I, 11) – and psychological contingencies are shown as if in a distorting mirror made to reflect one's distorting self back straight.

The natural world will allow itself to be darkened and quietened for a time, but then will realign its loyalties to a new cohort of gods, the Olympians. Such are the unbreakable laws of organic existence, including also, emphatically, the spiritual evolution that one senses is believed in by the poet: 'it must/Be of ripe progress' (I, 124-5). In this scheme of things, as if he has inscribed it in marble on behalf of the incoming gods, Keats tells us that the Titans have not got what it takes to admit the reality of, and therefore adapt to, the changing environment, so they naturally gravitate to minor roles. When the self-motivated Apollo arrives, the Titans are as far off and apathetic as tenured and timid staff-members in some moribund department of administration. Keats will not let a layer of dust settle on him like this: 'Scarce images of life, one here, one there,/Lay vast and edgeways; like a dismal cirque/Of Druid stones, upon a forlorn moor … '(II, 33-5). The gods (and their drones) of the past no longer exist as any part of the vital force of life. In Keats's time, science has killed the old gods and myths – or at any rate made the atmosphere unpropitious to them – so new ones have to be invented. Saturn and Thea are in what Keats has called, elsewhere, the 'Vale of Soul-making'

(*Letters*, I, p.102). In this region, 'cruel pain' (I, 44) is the stuff one must use to make one's soul. Titans refuse, and remain ignorant, and become angry. Hyperion himself is one such case:

> Fall! No, by Tellus and her briny robes!
> Over the fiery frontier of my realms
> I will advance a terrible right arm
> Shall scare that infant thunderer, rebel Jove,
> And bid old Saturn take his throne again. (I, 246-50)

Similarly, Saturn, in bewildered envy, hopes to create another world, but without in any way changing his approach:

> A little time, and then again he snatch'd
> Utterance thus. – 'But cannot I create?
> Cannot I form? Cannot I fashion forth
> Another world, another universe,
> To overbear and crumble this to naught?
> Where is another chaos? Where?' (I, 140-5)

One might be reminded of Lear and Kent unprepared for the new era in which Goneril and Regan acquired metaphorical serpents' teeth with which to see their hollowed father off once and for all. Saturn could scarcely survive, let alone triumph, in the 'fierce convulse' (III, 129) through which only the strong and properly prepared (because transformable) soul can 'Die into life' (III, 130). Keats has answered the call from his higher self, and his higher self has come to collect him: 'Soon wild commotions shook him, and made flush/All the immortal fairness of his limbs;/Most like the struggle at the gate of death … ' (III, 124-6). Many people refuse the call, because the realm from which it is sent to them is supposed not to exist. Sherlock Holmes would never bother about it. C.G. Jung (1875-1961) would bother about it, but, basically, he would be dismissed by the prevailing intellectualism of the twentieth century, despite arguing consistently that non-physical, psychic phenomena should be analysed as rigorously as physical phenomena. (Any intellectual conceding that non-physical, psychic phenomena are real runs the risk of being labelled unaccountably medieval – as if Diderot et al had not ridden roughshod over ancient puerilities.)

Hyperion, with all his hang ups, is the quintessence of the essentially healthy yet neurotic individual whose blackest thoughts are groundless (but have generated, for example, the Prozac and CBT phenomena that have busied an appreciable proportion of the western world's labour force, upon whose votes the political parties depend for their existence and power). With *Hyperion,* Keats wrote the Hyperion (the 'sober-sadness' he recognised in himself that he knew could be 'laughed at' with some justice [*Letters,* II, p.174]) out of himself. He said to Reynolds (on 3 May 1818) that 'until we are sick, we understand not; in fine, as Byron says, "Knowledge is sorrow", and I go on to say that "sorrow is wisdom". ' In the greatest poetry, personal and universal sufferings are inextricably combined. Keats knew that more, and stronger, pain was on its way to him. He eulogised it in advance. He knew the worms that would devour him had already hatched, so he saw to their – and many of the great mystery's other agents' – beautification.

9

'The Eve of St Agnes'

Some think I have lost that poetic ardour and fire 'tis said I once had – the fact is perhaps I have: but instead of that I hope I shall substitute a more thoughtful and quiet power. I am more frequently, now, contented to read and think – but now & then, haunted with ambitious thoughts. Qui[e]ter in my pulse, improved in my digestion; exerting myself against vexing speculations – scarcely content to write the best verses for the fever they leave behind. I want to compose without this fever. I hope I one day shall. (*Letters*, II, p.209)

The power and radiance of 'The Eve of St Agnes' seem to have left some key nineteenth- and twentieth-century commentators untouched. Jeffrey's synopsis of the poem is useful up to a point for its first-class succinctness:

The superstition is that if a maiden goes to bed on that night [St Agnes's Eve], without supper, and never looks up after saying her prayers, till she falls asleep, she will see her destined husband by her bedside the moment she opens her eyes. The fair Madeline, who was in love with the gentle Porphyro, but thwarted by an imperious guardian, resolves to try this spell: and Porphyro, who has a suspicion of her purpose, naturally determines to do what he can to help it to a happy issue; and accordingly prevails on her ancient nurse to admit him to her virgin bower; where he watches reverently, till she sinks in slumber; and then, arranging a most elegant dessert by her couch, and gently rousing her with a tender and favourite air, finally reveals himself, and persuades her to steal from the castle under his protection.

But such a summing-up can serve also to ironically display (in displaying Jeffrey's striking unawareness of it) the poem's abounding moral ambivalence. There is a sexual *frisson* in the poem, and the reader preferring his sensual nature to be left undisturbed may find Keats's key ingredient distasteful, or perhaps even distastefully delicious. Is it possible to read stanzas XXV and XXVI feelingly without indulging in a kind of voyeurism? Byron's jibe about 'this miserable Self-polluter of the human mind' (*Keats: The Critical Heritage*, p.129) was well-aimed (perhaps not least at Byron's own experience as a reader of 'The Eve of St Agnes'): 'such writing is a sort of mental masturbation … I don't mean he is *indecent*, but viciously soliciting his own ideas into a state, which is neither poetry nor any thing else but a Bedlam vision produced by raw pork and opium.' (*Keats: The Critical Heritage*, p.129) Perhaps even more worryingly (because more titillatingly?), the lovely Madeline is the unsuspecting performer, spied upon by Porphyro (and the reader) from the closet in the bedroom:

> Full on this casement shone the wintry moon,
> And threw warm gules on Madeline's fair breast,
> As down she knelt for heaven's grace and boon;
> Rose-bloom fell on her hands, together prest,
> And on her silver cross soft amethyst,
> And on her hair a glory, like a saint:
> She seem'd a splendid angel, newly drest,
> Save wings, for heaven: – Porphyro grew faint:
> She knelt, so pure a thing, so free from mortal taint. (XXV)

The contemporary reader may have found in the above stanza what Coleridge called the 'vicious taste of our modern … Monk Lewis' (*Coleridge Notebooks*, 3449). Coleridge had in mind Matthew Lewis (1775-1818), whose sensational Gothic novel, *The Monk* (1796), contained many passages suggesting irresistibly that the author had been shockingly transfixed by his own violent, youthful aching for female flesh:

> … [Matilda] lifted her arm, and made a motion as if to stab
> herself. The friar's eyes followed with dread the course of the
> dagger. She had torn open her habit, and her bosom was half
> exposed. The weapon's point rested upon her left breast: and, oh!
> that was such a breast! The moon-beams darting full upon it
> enabled the monk to observe its dazzling whiteness: his eye dwelt

with insatiable avidity upon the beauteous orb: a sensation till
then unknown filled his heart with a mixture of anxiety and
delight; a raging fire shot through every limb; the blood boiled
in his veins, and a thousand wild wishes bewildered his
imagination. (*The Monk*, Vol. I, Ch. II)

The intentions of Keats's Porphyro do not appear to be as bad – but this
too could be self-deception:

> 'I will not harm her; by all saints I swear,'
> Quoth Porphyro: 'O may I ne'er find grace
> 'When my weak voice shall whisper its last prayer;
> 'If one of her soft ringlets I displace,
> 'Or look with ruffian passion in her face … (XVII).

That is, it is better to look through a keyhole. However, rather
unsettlingly, Porphyro's feelings are clear, without his intentions being
clearly defined. The lack of definition is part of the point. The reader's
experience of Keats's best poetry depends upon incomplete and
uncertain knowledge. Remember Homer, aloof in giant ignorance.
Remember that Shakespeare never advises readers whether his Hamlet,
or his Richard III, is good or bad. Keats's works, like Shakespeare's, are
distinguished by the conspicuous absence of moral directives. The
'poetical Character,' says Keats, 'has as much delight in conceiving an Iago
as an Imogen. What shocks the virtuous philosopher, delights the
chameleon Poet. It does no harm from its relish of the dark side of things
any more than from its taste for the bright one.' Madeline performs a
striptease without knowing it:

> Anon his heart revives: her vespers done,
> Of all its wreathed pearls her hair she frees;
> Unclasps her warmed jewels one by one;
> Loosens her fragrant bodice; by degrees
> Her rich attire creeps rustling to her knees:
> Half-hidden, like a mermaid in sea-weed … (XXVI).

Is there not something silkily, and sinfully, indulgent about what Jack
Stillinger would call 'the line-by-line richness' (*The Wordsworth Circle*,
XXXVIII, No. 3, 139) of the above passage? Dare one enjoy the passage
as a porously receptive reader? Or would one have to emerge in shame

from the experience? The poem is a guilty pleasure.

Keats has draped the boundaries of good taste with sweet-scented Spenserian stanzas, and it is harder for the reader to perceive precisely how the boundaries are being pushed, or dissolved – though s/he does sense that they are being changed in some way. Having written his way through strange psychic territories where personal and universal concerns overlap, Keats now has the practiced boldness to generate a sort of verbal Eden. Is there not a serpent present too? The poem is intensely erotic. 'The Imagination may be compared to Adam's dream – he awoke and found it truth.' (*Letters*, I, p.185) Can the fumes of a personal Hell be detected through the poppied air of 'The Eve of St Agnes'? A letter from Keats to Benjamin Bailey (July 1818) is remarkably revealing:

> I am certain I have not a right feeling towards Women – at this moment I am striving to be just to them but I cannot – Is it because they fall so far beneath my Boyish imagination? When I was a Schoolboy I though[t] a fair Woman a pure Goddess, my mind was a soft nest in which some one of them slept though she knew it not – I have no right to expect more than their reality. I thought them etherial above Men – I find them perhaps equal – great by comparison is very small – Insult may be inflicted in more ways than by Word or action – one who is tender of being insulted does not like to think an insult against another – I do not like to think insults in a Lady's Company – I commit a Crime with her which absence would have not known – Is it not extraordinary? When among men I have no evil thoughts, no malice, no spleen – I feel free to speak or to be silent – I can listen and from everyone I can learn – my hands are in my pockets I am free from all suspicion and comfortable. When I am among Women I have evil thoughts, malice, spleen – I cannot speak or be silent – I am full of Suspicions and therefore listen to no thing – I am in a hurry to be gone – You must be charitable and put all this perversity to my being disappointed since Boyhood ... (*Letters*, I, p.341).

Whether or not one forgets that one is, at some level, spying (with Porphyro) on Madeline, it is difficult to envisage a more prodigiously dreamlike – and at the same time delicately precise – combination of words with which to recreate the occasion of a beautiful young girl getting into a cold bed, heating it with her own body warmth, and going to sleep:

> Soon, trembling in her soft and chilly nest,
> In sort of wakeful swoon, perplex'd she lay,
> Until the poppied warmth of sleep oppress'd
> Her soothed limbs, and soul fatigued away;
> Flown, like a thought, until the morrow-day
> Blissfully haven'd both from joy and pain;
> Clasped like a missal where swart Paynims pray.
> Blinded alike from sunshine and from rain,
> As though a rose should shut, and be a bud again. (XXVII)

Perhaps Porphyro (like his creator, not wanting 'to think insults in a Lady's Company' but thinking them nevertheless?) is in some sense the serpent:

> Stol'n to this paradise, and so entranced,
> Porphyro gazed upon her empty dress,
> And listen'd to her breathing, if it chanced
> To wake into a slumberous tenderness;
> Which when he heard, that minute did he bless,
> And breath'd himself: then from the closet crept,
> Noiseless as fear in a wide wilderness,
> And over the hush'd carpet, silent, stept,
> And 'tween the curtains peep'd, where, lo! – how fast she slept. (XXVIII)

The depth of Keats's appreciation for Book IV of *Paradise Lost*, in which Satan gazes in unhappiness at Adam and Eve's uncorrupted circumstances, is clear:

> Under a tuft of shade that on a green
> Stood whispering soft, by a fresh fountain side
> They sat them down, and after no more toil
> Of their sweet gardening labour than sufficed
> To recommend cool zephyr, and made ease
> More easy, wholesome thirst and appetite
> More grateful, to their supper fruits they fell,
> Nectarine fruits which the compliant boughs
> Yielded them, sidelong as they sat recline
> On the soft downy bank damasked with flowers:
> The savoury pulp they chew, and in the rind

Still as they thirsted scoop the brimming stream ...
(*Paradise Lost*, IV, 325-36).

The fragrant textures in Keats's versification are Miltonic:

And still she slept an azure-lidded sleep,
In blanched linen, smooth, and lavender'd,
While he from forth the closet brought a heap
Of candied apple, quince, and plum, and gourd;
With jellies soother than the creamy curd,
And lucent syrops, tinct with cinnamon;
Manna and dates, in argosy transferr'd
From Fez; and spiced dainties, every one,
From silken Samarcand to cedar'd Lebanon. (XXX)

The word 'dainties' – used, less felicitously, not so long ago in stanza XLVII of 'Isabella' – is now an integral part of one of the mature poet's truly great works. Keats does not waste words now, much less deploy them to unwittingly comic effect. Even the above adjective-rich ('spiced', 'silken', 'cedar'd') passage does not cloy, possibly because Samarkand (one of the oldest cities of Asia, once the capital of Tamerlane's Mongol empire) and Lebanon (part of the Ottoman Empire from the early sixteenth century, and with a coastline on the Mediterranean Sea) are ingredients too far-flung to blend in the mind as Carlyle's alleged 'world of treacle!'

Arguably, Keats's 'Life of Sensations' (*Letters*, I, p.185) heightens the reader's sensual pleasure whilst simultaneously etherising his morals. Porphyro gets into bed with Madeline:

Beyond a mortal man impassion'd far
At these voluptuous accents, he arose,
Ethereal, flush'd, and like a throbbing star
Seen mid the sapphire heaven's deep repose;
Into her dream he melted, as the rose
Blendeth its odour with the violet, –
Solution sweet ... (XXXVI).

He seems to make love to her. Is it rape? The reader has been inundated with 'woofed phantasies' and 'voluptuous accents', and may feel more inclined to 'look ... dreamingly' than judge soberly. The presence of a sort of narcoleptic cocoon inhabited by Madeline and Porphyro (and the reader) is somehow confirmed, rather than dispelled, by the pattering upon it of 'the flaw-blown sleet'. The experience so far is of haziness, warmth, and low-level sexual tension, like the increasingly unfocused masturbation of a young man (Keats?) about to fall asleep. The reader does not have to strain to imagine why Byron sneered at 'Johnny Keats's *p-ss a bed* poetry.'

Madeline and Porphyro escape from the castle, and in the process the reader is treated to a masterful display of familiar Gothic scenery. The restless chilly breezes agitate the castle's interior, including the lamplight, the hanging embroidery and the carpeting:

> She hurried at his words, beset with fears,
> For there were sleeping dragons all around,
> At glaring watch, perhaps, with ready spears –
> Down the wide stairs a darkling way they found.–
> In all the house was heard no human sound.
> A chain-droop'd lamp was flickering by each door;
> The arras, rich with horseman, hawk, and hound,
> Flutter'd in the besieging wind's uproar;
> And the long carpets rose along the gusty floor. (XL)

Against this backdrop, the momentum of the spectral, escaping lovers – and the images and sounds accompanying their flight – is almost cinematic:

> They glide, like phantoms, into the wide hall;
> Like phantoms, to the iron porch, they glide;
> Where lay the porter in uneasy sprawl,
> With a huge empty flagon by his side:
> The wakeful bloodhound rose, and shook his hide,
> But his sagacious eye an inmate owns:
> By one, and one, the bolts full easy slide: –
> The chains lie silent on the footworn stones; –
> The key turns, and the door upon its hinges groans. (XLI)

Now that the lovers – the dreamers – have gone from the castle, death and decay (the 'large coffin-worm' and the 'ashes cold') close in like Blake's, or Shelley's, shades of death:

Death is here, and death is there,
Death is busy everywhere,
All around, within, beneath,
Above, is death – and we are death …

First our pleasures die – and then
Our hopes, and then our fears – and when
These are dead, the debt is due,
Dust claims dust – and we die too.

All things that we love and cherish,
Like ourselves, must fade and perish;
Such is our rude mortal lot –
Love itself would, did they not. (Shelley, 'Death')

We are left with nothing but the story, and, most importantly, how that story has been told. Of old Angela, the Baron and the Beadsman posterity can only have the names. (It looks unlikely that there will be any records.) Despite the warm and sensible motions of those who dance and drink and sing 'Amid the timbrels, and the throng'd resort/Of whisperers in anger, or in sport;/'Mid looks of love, defiance, hate, and scorn' (VIII), the vast majority of them is 'Hoodwink'd with faery fancy', chasing 'all the bliss to be', instead of finding fulfilment in the moment, now: 'Sudden a thought came like a full-blown rose,/Flushing his brow, and in his pained heart/Made purple riot … ' (XVI). In these lines, the thought that suddenly occurs to Porphyro is that he will persuade Angela to sneak him into Madeline's bedroom; but, of course, the thought has occurred to Porphyro's creator, the poet with the dendritic imagination to feel the mucky provenance – not just see the nice effect – of a 'full-blown rose'. The poet is now writing consistently at his best; and further, the poetry his pen has yet to glean from his teeming brain will not need to be explainable to be immortal. 'The faint conceptions I have of Poems to come brings the blood frequently into my forehead'.

10

'Ode to a Nightingale'

To some readers, Keats's state of mind after writing *Hyperion* can seem as lacking in robustness as it did beforehand. In 'Ode to a Nightingale' (1819), having complained that 'My heart aches, and a drowsy numbness pains/My sense, as though of hemlock I had drunk', Keats claims to 'have been half in love with easeful Death,/Call'd him soft names in many a mused rhyme,/To take into the air my quiet breath'. Why 'half in love'? The young poet is like most of us, in that he keenly feels the pain of consciousness and yet has not entirely objective grounds for putting an end to his existence. Keats has by now absorbed and accommodated the 'death wish' as many people do. As a great poet, he has anatomised it even as it has melted and mutated in the most fugitive mode.

Not all readers have had the patience (or courage) to follow half-thoughts through the shades of grey evoked – or invoked – by Keats. Could he not have tried to define his negative emotions more sharply? This is what Sylvia Plath (1932-63) would do, with the result that many readers would avert their gaze in horror, though prepared to recognise Plath's disturbed brilliance. The delight of seeing Keats achieving such a grasp of his unalterable personal circumstances is not cancelled by the terrible nature of those circumstances and his use of them as a poet. Yes, Keats has a very sore throat when writing the poem, but his 'light-winged Dryad of the trees' sings 'of summer in full-throated ease.' The poet, like some kind of metaphysical amphibian, or, for that matter, like a shaman, can inhabit his sore-throated or full-throated self almost at will; he can 'Fade far away, dissolve, and quite forget' (rather like the Titans in *Hyperion*) the pain that flesh is heir to, or he can remain present and improvable.

There are passages in this poem whose omission would not have seemed to damage the central theme, but which can touch and transform the reader, as if in passing, like the hem of some wonderful garment flowing behind a blessed saviour, or a ritual magician, on the move. For example, in

O for a beaker full of the warm South,
   Full of the true, the blushful Hippocrene,
     With beaded bubbles winking at the brim,
       And purple-stained mouth

the reader can see a whole evening of drinking, and how enjoyable such an evening can seem *at the time* is encapsulated with pristine empathy – and yet one also recognises, if one is honest with oneself, that one has often acquired a purple-stained mouth in pursuit of a few hours' peace from pain- and death-related emotions.

Keats explores a state of mind known to anyone who has ever wanted to – while at the same time knowing they cannot – retreat from the world. The desire to 'Fade far away, dissolve' echoes Hamlet's wish to 'melt,/Thaw, and resolve … into a dew' (Act I, scene 2, 29-30), and foreshadows Thomas Hood's (1799-1845) *Bridge of Sighs* (1844), which Charles Baudelaire (1821-67) translated, finding in it the phrase 'Anywhere out of the world' to borrow as the title for a prose poem of his own. Baudelaire expressed his vision of the world as a hospital ward with brilliant bitterness. But the same human predicament as expressed by Keats has no mention of a hospital, and yet a whole ward-full of suffering is revealed in one glance at the convex reflection of one of his freshly-beaded lyric teardrops: 'The weariness, the fever, and the fret/Here where men sit and hear each other groan' (III). The reader instinctively knows that the writer capable of generating a panoptic moment such as this one will have the power and magic to create yet more mental spaciousness.

Symbolically, the bird is inextinguishable ('Thou wast not born for death, immortal Bird!'), beyond the reach of human destructiveness and rapacity ('No hungry generations tread thee down'). Again, Keats provides a miniature picture – this time a flash from the remote past – which magically presents the nightingale's perennial quintessence: 'The voice I hear this passing night was heard/In ancient days by emperor and clown'. Magic showings have usurped empirical evidence in this stanza (VII), which culminates in Keats's bird being said to have 'Charm'd magic casements, opening on the foam/Of perilous seas, in faery lands forlorn.' The alliteration itself foams, and the feel of the poet's language has become almost completely immersive, almost as if we could stay there forever. But – and this is an important part of the point – we are not there, and it will only be a matter of time before some happenstance word, in the very flow of words required to promote the mood and contrive the vision, will puncture and pucker the whole seductive sphere, letting the atmosphere of the unimaginative world back in. For Keats, 'forlorn' does it: 'Forlorn! the very word is like a bell/To toll me back from thee to my sole self!' Just as the flaw-blown sleet pattering on the windowpane gave heightened definition to the vision involving Madeline and Porphyro in 'The Eve of St Agnes', so the return to diminished consciousness from poetic vision in 'Ode to a Nightingale' serves to enhance the otherworldly colour and power. The bell-sound grows: 'forlorn' – with its small f at the end of stanza VII, and swelling to 'Forlorn!' at the beginning of the concluding stanza with a capital F and an exclamation mark. Similarly, the fading from the vision is represented by 'Adieu! adieu!', and one is not quite sure whether it is the vision or the speaker himself who is retreating 'Up the hill-side' like unaccountable Lakeland vapours. The ambivalence the reader is left with is lingeringly provocative: 'Fled is that music: – Do I wake or sleep?' There is no moral pressure at any point. (The pressure of being mortal, however, needles the poet's attention like a fishbone.) Vapours and visions come and go as they will, when they will, and Keats knows that however strenuously some of his contemporaries might squint for a desired result, Shakespeare was always clear- and open-eyed – yet knowing that even supreme clarity and openness is no guarantee of any human being's actual independence from the binding mammalian dream.

Drug, or alcohol, addiction can be an avoidance of mortality – 'Now more than ever seems it rich to die,/To cease upon the midnight with no pain' – and Keats's sense of his own mortality, particularly since expectorating and recognising his own arterial blood during a tubercular coughing-fit in February 1820 (*Letters*, II, p.251 and p.254), would give him anything but ease.

11

'Ode on Indolence'

Keats could also find opulent expression for his most lethargic moods, as in the following stanza from 'Ode On Indolence':

> They faded, and, forsooth! I wanted wings:
>   O folly! What is love! and where is it?
> And for that poor Ambition! it springs
>   From a man's little heart's short fever-fit;
> For Poesy! – no, – she has not a joy, –
>   At least for me, – so sweet as drowsy noons,
>   And evenings steep'd in honied indolence;
> O, for an age so shelter'd from annoy,
>   That I may never know how change the moons,
>   Or hear the voice of busy common-sense!

A man of character is, by his very nature, 'incapable of remaining Content with half-knowledge' (*Letters*, I, p.194). For Keats, Wordsworth was a man of character, preaching from within his impressive – but in the end wooden and unworkable – system of thought. By 1817-18, Keats's imaginative orientation in the direction of the unspecific – his glorious courage of his lack of conviction – took shape, and it is as if there emerged over his art the transformative power of a new sunrise, leaving in shade what his art was not: 'We hate poetry that has a palpable design upon us – and if we do not agree, seems to put its hand in its breeches pocket. Poetry should be great & unobtrusive, a thing which enters into one's soul, and does not startle it or amaze it with itself but with its subject. – How beautiful are the retired flowers! how they would lose their beauty were they to throng into the highway crying out, "admire me I am a violet! dote upon me I am a primrose!" ' (*Letters*, I, p.224) In anatomising his own talent and temperament, Keats continued to reaffirm that he had more in common with Shakespeare – 'Chief Poet!'

(*Letters*, I, p.215) – than with Wordsworth: 'Modern poets differ from the Elizabethans in this. Each of the moderns like an Elector of Hanover governs his petty state, & knows how many straws are swept daily from the Causeways in all his dominions … I will cut all this – I will have no more of Wordsworth … why should we kick against the Pricks, when we can walk on Roses? … – Why with Wordsworth's "Matthew with a bough of wilding in his hand" when we can have Jacques [from Shakespeare's *As You Like It*, Act II, scene 1, 31] "under an oak &c" … ' (*Letters*, I, p.224).

In his copy of Milton's (1608-74) *Paradise Lost* (1667-74), Keats made some notes: 'What creates the intense pleasure of not knowing? A sense of independence, of power, from the fancy's creating a world of its own by the sense of probabilities.' (Gittings, p.262.) Books IV and VII of *Paradise Lost* – 'two specimens of very extraordinary beauty … better described in themselves than by a volume' (Gittings, pp.262-3) – boosted Keats's imagination in a way that no other writing apart from Shakespeare's could: 'Nothing is finer for the purposes of great productions, than a very gradual ripening of the intellectual powers … ' (*Letters*, I, p.214).

To denigrate Keats on the grounds that he had no character – or at any rate not enough character to rank alongside the greatest poets – would involve forgetting all about the greatest poets, namely Milton and Shakespeare. Keats knew this, and could articulate it in his prose as clearly and magically as he could create his poetry: ' … several things dovetailed in my mind, & at once it struck me, what quality went to form a Man of Achievement especially in Literature & which Shakespeare possessed so enormously – I mean *Negative Capability*, that is when a man is capable of being in uncertainties, Mysteries, doubts, without any irritable reaching after fact & reason … ' (*Letters*, I, p.193). Keats's '*Negative Capability*' involves passive achievement – a suspension of judgment so that ideas and feelings can be creatively explored. Keats's letters refer to the various 'Chambers' of his own imagination which, when it received sense impressions from the outside world, could produce poetry as organically as 'the Leaves of a tree' (*Letters*, I, p.238). He felt that he was tapping into a power that all humans had in them, but very few (except, for example, Shakespeare) realised. 'Now it appears to me that almost any Man may like the spider spin from his own inwards his own airy Citadel – the points of the leaves and twigs on which the spider begins her work are few, and she fills the air with a beautiful circuiting: man should be content with as few points to top with the fine Webb of his Soul and weave a tapestry empyrean – full of Symbols for his spiritual eye, of softness for his spiritual touch, of space for his wandering of distinctness for his Luxury.' (*Letters*, I, pp.231-2) He knew himself, in the fullest sense of the phrase – physiologically and temperamentally, as the following exegesis of an isolated episode of his own 'laziness' shows:

> This morning I am in a sort of temper indolent and supremely careless: I long after a stanza or two of Thompson's Castle of indolence – My passions are all asleep from my having slumbered till nearly eleven and weakened the animal fibre all over me to a delightful sensation about three degrees on this side of faintness – if I have teeth of pearl and the breath of lilies I should call it languor – but as I am … I must call it Laziness – In this state of effeminacy the fibres of the brain are relaxed in common with the rest of the body, and to such a happy degree that pleasure has no show of enticement and pain no unbearable frown. Neither Poetry, nor Ambition, nor Love have any alertness of countenance as they pass by me: they seem rather like three figures on a greek vase – a Man and two women – whom no one but myself could distinguish in their disguisement. This is the only happiness; and is a rare instance of advantage in the body overpowering the Mind. (*Letters*, II, pp.78-9)

One thinks of Keats's 'Ode on a Grecian Urn' as etched in marble, so it feels like an unusual pleasure to catch a glimpse of 'a greek vase' in prose pre-dating that ode.

As he continued to feel his poetic potential gathering in him, Keats's anxieties about the past or the future did not, he said, contaminate the purity of his contemplation. He wrote to Benjamin Bailey in November 1817: 'you perhaps at one time thought there was such a thing as Worldly Happiness to be arrived at, at certain periods of time marked out – you have of necessity from your disposition been thus led away – I scarcely remember counting upon any Happiness – I look not for it if it be not in the present hour – nothing startles me beyond the Moment.' (*Letters*, I, p.186) He wanted to savour each moment, to live in it, not through it. How many of today's enthusiasts of Eckhart Tolle (1948-), recently released from remorse about the past and anxiety about the future, and intoxicated on 'the power of now', are aware that such ideas were formulated – though by no means originated – by Keats? 'When Man has arrived at a certain ripeness in intellect any one grand and spiritual passage serves him as a starting post towards all "the two-and thirty Pallaces". How happy is such a "voyage of conception", what delicious diligent Indolence! A doze upon a sofa does not hinder it, and a nap upon Clover engenders ethereal finger-pointings' (*Letters*, I, pp.231-2).

According to Richard Woodhouse, Keats had only to see a billiard ball in order to 'conceive … that it may have a sense of delight from its own roundness, smoothness volubility & the rapidity of its motion' (Bate, p.261). Keats could accept the incomplete knowledge that 'Beauty is truth, truth beauty' as 'all [he needed] to know', without attempting to orientate the insight any further in order to meet any intellectual impatience on its own terms: 'I have an idea that a Man might pass a very pleasant life in this manner – let him on any certain day read a certain Page of full Poesy or distilled Prose, and let him wander with it, and muse upon it, and reflect from it, and bring home to it, and prophesy upon it, and dream upon it' (*Letters*, I, pp.231-2). Keats could dilate even the smallest chamber of mental freedom into a dreamscape. But such a dreamscape will no more interest literal-minded people than the topographical realities of Holland will interest mountaineers.

12

'Ode on a Grecian Urn'

Following Blake's example of the interrogative, exclamatory approach in a poem ('Did he who made the lamb make thee?'), Keats asks questions too, but of what or whom it is unclear: it is not the case that he is actually affecting to ask the Grecian urn itself – 'What men or gods are these? What maidens loth?/What mad pursuit? What struggle to escape?/What pipes and timbrels? What wild ecstasy?' – about the scenes depicted on it. Rather, the urn serves as the medium for the expression of a mode of life and culture long vanished, yet still accessible to the open, dreaming mind touchable by poetry. Just as a new 'planet' can swim into one's ken (but not one's control), so too can music seem to find its way to a point just beyond the reach, and the perishing touch, of 'the sensual ear'. Keats, for all his self-knowledge, is still experiencing some revulsion for the inescapable, irreversible process of change and decay – the arrow of time. In indulging that fearful, futile Hyperion-self still in him, he can also watch it as it welcomes each static scene depicted on the urn as some sort of suggestion of the possibility of literally stopping the arrow of time. The fearful, yearning self in Keats – in us all – then relishes the imaginary prospect of a changeless universe in which, for example, one's lover's personal beauty remains eternally intact, or one never wearies of, say, music, or the company of one's lover, and one never has to see the leaves falling from the trees telling one that winter is on its way. Again, the profusion of imagery becomes immersive, and it is almost as if the reader has become a naturalised inhabitant of this strange dimension where nothing changes, looking back almost with pity at 'All breathing human passions' which leave poor mortals 'high-sorrowful and cloy'd', their foreheads 'burning' and their tongues 'parching'.

Planets are left pockmarked, or even destroyed utterly, by the impacts of other huge, hurling, whirling lumps in space. The human body inherits what Shakespeare calls the thousand natural shocks. Any attempt to avoid the pockmarks, the shocks or the ultimate destruction of one's self as one thinks one knows it is as certain of failing as trying to make a square triangle, or even trying to imagine one. The arrow of time cannot be reversed, or stopped, and Keats – for all his searching and shape-shifting between warm mammal and 'Cold Pastoral', between 'truth' and 'beauty' – is, of course, unable to shift anything outside his own dream.

What is there, though, outside the dream – the poetic vision – worth bothering about?

13

'Bright Star! Would I Were Steadfast as Thou Art!'

In this poem Keats's star, like the scenes on the urn, looks 'steadfast' – something that we poor human beings, forced to ride the roller-coaster of emotions and then die, can never be. Keats, however, is a true poet, and so his *aspiration* to be steadfast is troubling in its burning intensity. 'I have felt/A presence that disturbs me with the joy/Of elevated thoughts,' said Wordsworth in his 'Lines Written a Few Miles above Tintern Abbey' (1798), in which he expressed his deep love for his sister. Keats too expresses his love for Fanny Brawne, but whereas Wordsworth had recognised something of his former self in the shooting lights of Dorothy's wild eyes, Keats is contemplating abdicating (remember Lear) his former self in order simply to be 'Pillow'd upon my fair love's ripening breast,/To feel for ever its soft fall and swell,/Awake for ever in a sweet unrest,/Still, still to hear her tender-taken breath,/And so live ever – or else swoon to death.' The desire to regress into childhood innocence is what Keats is observing in himself. It is not a desire that has taken possession of him entirely. He is demonstrating his uncanny capacity for ambivalent attention to his own doubleness. He is at once like one of the figures on the urn, 'for ever' with his head resting childishly on his lover's bosom, *and* the higher, brighter other co-ordinate to which humanity will owe the debt of gratitude.

14

'This Living Hand'

One may be reminded of Porphyro's 'glowing hand' in stanza XXXI of 'The Eve of St Agnes' (and his unsettlingly vague intentions in Madeline's bedroom), and one may also catch a verbal echo of Shakespeare's Claudio expressing his fear of death to his sister Isabella: 'To lie in cold obstruction and to rot;/This sensible warm motion to become/A kneaded clod … ' (*Measure For Measure*, Act III, scene 1, 122-4). The tyrannical Angelo has told Isabella that if she refuses to grant him his sexual wishes, he will have Claudio killed. On hearing of this, Claudio is understandably keen for Isabella to prioritise his life above her own virtue. As it happens, she does not. This is another wintry blast of Shakespearean wisdom. Actions and destinies are determined by characters' own flawed passions and points of view. Isabella (reacting to her brother's 'cowardice'), like Cordelia (reacting to her father's foolish request for verbal confirmation of her love for him), is trying to do the right thing – but the reader is never told what is really 'right'. Fanny Brawne's refusal to comply with Keats's wishes may echo, for the poet, Shakespeare's revelations. If this is the case, then the pressure of meaning behind the following words has resonances of Claudio's pressure on Isabella, and Lear's on Cordelia: 'thou would wish thine own heart dry of blood/So in my veins red life might stream again,/And thou be conscience-calm'd … '. However, Keats completes this short poem with an extraordinary gesture of his 'living hand': '– see here it is –/I hold it towards you.' It feels as if the gesture is made towards the reader of distant posterity – as if the hand is being outstretched, not just through time and space, but through the dream connecting readers and writers scattered in time and space – indeed the dream we all live in – by way of a greeting. James Elroy Flecker (1884-1915) would surely find in this symbol the inspiration to write 'To a Poet a Thousand Years Hence':

O friend unseen, unborn, unknown,
Student of our sweet English tongue,
Read out my words at night, alone:
I was a poet, I was young.

Since I can never see your face,
And never shake you by the hand,
I send my soul through time and space
To greet you. You will understand.

15

'Ode to Psyche'

Psyche is the goddess of the soul, and Keats's ode to her is a warm act of advocacy for the least worshipped divine being in the Greek pantheon. No longer is the poet apologising ('Like a sick eagle looking at the sky') for his interest in Greek ideas: 'Yet even in these days so far retir'd/From happy pieties … I see, and sing, by my own eyes inspir'd.' There is an enriching ambivalence about the means with which he has had his vision: 'Surely I dreamt to-day, or did I see/The winged Psyche with awaken'd eyes?' The levelling of dreams and waking thought is not second, but first, nature to the poet. There is no discernible anxiety to show that he has outgrown his cockney contemporary. He remains in Hunt's debt: the 'hush'd, cool-rooted flowers, fragrant-eyed,/Blue, silver-white, and budded Tyrian' could easily have been found in *The Story of Rimini*. But the power and compactness is his own, and he has, by the time of writing this first of his great odes, in April 1819, become what Shelley will say (in his *Defence of Poetry*, 1821) a true poet is – a hierophant of unapprehended wisdom: 'Yes, I will be thy priest, and build a fane/In some untrodden region of my mind,/Where branched thoughts, new growth with pleasant pain,/Instead of pines shall murmur in the wind … '. Eight lines after 'pain', there emerges 'the wreath'd trellis of a working brain'. Those eight lines could represent the 'Vale of Soul-making' in which personal suffering has been approached as the raw material and worked into the worthiness of the poet *par excellence*.

The poem has an achieved greatness accompanied by a giddiness of vision comparable with Shelley's 'Triumph of Life' (1822). Shelley: 'All flowers, in field or forest, which unclose/Their trembling eyelids to the kiss of day,/Swinging their censers in the element,/With orient incense lit by the new ray/Burned slow and inconsumably, and sent/Their odorous sighs up to the smiling air … '. Keats: 'Thy voice, thy lute, thy pipe, thy incense sweet/From swinged censer teeming;/Thy shrine, thy grove, thy oracle, thy heat/Of pale-mouth'd prophet dreaming.' Shelley's rite of the morning is *observed* – by the Sun, the ocean, the birds, and even the 'smiling' air. Keats's rite is similarly 'Holy', and similarly unencumbered by the impostures of Christianity. Keats demanded of himself – his individuality and his use of personal suffering – 'a greater system of salvation than the Christian religion.' Hunt had attacked, in journalism, the Prince Regent, but Keats was attacking, in poetry, the religion of the Establishment. He had already done this in, for example, his sonnet 'Written in Disgust of Vulgar Superstition' ('Surely the mind of man is closely bound/In some black spell'), but now he was throwing back the curtain to reveal a genuinely uplifting alternative.

16

'Fancy'

No proper Christian could 'Open wide the mind's cage-door' (7) in order to let Fancy 'dart forth, and cloudward soar.' (8)

> Every thing is spoilt by use:
> Where's the cheek that doth not fade,
> Too much gaz'd at? Where's the maid
> Whose lip mature is ever new?
> Where's the eye, however blue,
> Doth not weary? Where's the face
> One would meet in every place?
> Where's the voice, however soft,
> One would hear so very oft?
> At a touch sweet Pleasure melteth …

There is the sense, from the above roster of grievances, that one is chained to the material world with the same sorrowful resignation as a husband is to a wife, or a wife to a husband. Initially, one was enchanted, and one's most urgent desire was to get as close as possible to the object of one's fixation and secure possession. Sooner or later, however, one is forced to realise that possession has indeed been secured – that is, one is in possession of the world/spouse, and joy evaporates as petty miseries flourish in the forcing-house from which poetry is excluded. ('Pleasure never is at home.') There remains the prospect of transgression: for the prisoner of marriage, 'a mistress', and for the prisoner of the material world, 'sweet Fancy!' Conscious oppression, unconscious oppression, and the tyranny of the unimaginative have driven many individuals ever more deeply into inner-space. Though attempts have been made, with some success, to control it – once by authoritarian Christianity and nowadays by ingratiating and ever more immersive information technologies – the imagination cannot be controlled. This is why expressions of imagination are derided and marginalised by Establishment values. If the visions of a young cockney were to be taken seriously, where on earth would London, and Britain, be?

17

'Ode to Autumn'

He had looked up into the night sky, and he had looked into Chapman's Homer, and found – himself: 'Then felt I like some watcher of the skies/When a new planet swims into his ken'. It is significant to remember that one of the passages of Chapman's Homer that most excited Keats involved the planet Jupiter rising in an *Autumn* sky.

Now, in 'Ode to Autumn', the 'I' – the personal pronoun – has been shed like a full-grown and withered leaf, because the poet is prepared to see life's deciduousness through in order to transcend it by accessing – and even himself becoming – a special kind of objectivity. It is an objectivity that, unlike the kind taught by the French *philosophes*, does not aspire to absolute detachment from, or superiority to, the individual experience of the material world and its wearisome, feverish and fretful irrationalities. As merely descriptive poetry, 'Ode to Autumn' is famously sensual and vivid: many readers will savour the 'mists and mellow fruitfulness', the 'hair soft-lifted by the winnowing wind', and the 'wailful choir' of 'small gnats' that mourns 'Among the river sallows, borne aloft/Or sinking as the light wind lives or dies'. But this poetry promotes an osmosis of feeling and meaning in the mutual involvement of personal and universal concerns. The year – like the writer, to say nothing of the reader – is dying. The flourishing features of the physical world suggest some source of their own nourishment that is metaphysical.

In this zone of consciousness, reality that is not material is given definition it does not often enjoy in the industrializing culture Keats finds himself living in: 'Where are the songs of Spring? Ay, where are they?' (They are in the imagination, or nowhere.) 'Hedge-crickets sing', the 'red-breast whistles' and 'gathering swallows twitter in the skies.' Remember, the year is dying. But there is an impulse (symbolised by the mysteriously energised swallows) to move out of the gathering shadow of death – to go south, like Porphyro and Madeline. When one is sick, one may long (though perhaps in vain) to get well, even as one gets worse. If the reader of the poem is familiar with Keats's personal circumstances, the phrase 'Thou watchest the last oozings hours by hours' might bring to mind Joseph Severn's sketch of the poet on his deathbed, and the artist's note below that sketch: '28 Janry 3 o'clock mng. Drawn to keep me awake – a deadly sweat was on him all this night'.

Part of the poet's point is that everything that lives dies. Gnats die, and humans die, but sensed in the special atmosphere of Keats's zone of symbols, the 'choir' of one species is no more affectingly 'wailful' than the choir of the other. We do not think small gnats ever mourn. The question provoked in us by the poem is not, however, What do we think gnats do? but What do we think we do? ('Think not of them'.) Medieval man saw himself in all things and all things in himself, bearing, this 'correspondence within him', as Jung would put it, 'by virtue of his reflecting consciousness, on the one hand, and, on the other, thanks to the hereditary, archetypal nature of his instincts, which bind him to his environment.' (*The Undiscovered Self*, 1958) 'Enlightened' intellectuals will scorn any idea that the appearance of a comet in the sky has anything to do with the squabbles and other trivialities on earth: is it not my boundless ego, ignorance and vanity that prompt me to write into my own story the distant flight of a thunderbolt? No. And 'Ode to Autumn' shows why not.

The sun is not maturing; the year is, and I am. But like Wallace Stevens's (1879-1955) blackbird, the sun 'is involved in what I know', whether I am a thirteenth-century peasant or the most up-to-date astronomer. When Shelley called Keats 'a portion of that loveliness/Which once he made more lovely', he had in mind the imperishable radiance Keats never failed to behold beyond all perishable things – including his own autumnal, tubercular body.

18

'Ode on Melancholy'

One of Keats's great odes was to the Greek goddess, Psyche. Another was to a Greek vase. Another was to a season – autumn. Another was to a bird – the nightingale. 'Ode on Melancholy' shows the poet opening some metaphorical casements on a mood that, like the sea, has been much written about yet still remains mysterious. Melancholy can come as suddenly as a storm-blast on the Ancient Mariner's ocean: 'the melancholy fit shall fall/Sudden from heaven like a weeping cloud'. Or it can, more gradually, turn 'aching Pleasure … to Poison'. Where does it come from? Where does it go to? Any answer, of course, is not located in space and time – and the only way an answer could be conceived is in terms of some of the familiar specifics of the material world – such as yew-berries and peonies (not to mention the familiar specifics of literary culture such as Lethe and Proserpine):

> Make not your rosary of yew-berries,
> Nor let the beetle, nor the death-moth be
> Your mournful Psyche, nor the downy owl
> A partner in your sorrow's mysteries.

Keats does not want to 'drown the wakeful anguish of the soul', because, however unpleasant, this is the medium in which transformation happens. If you 'go … to Lethe', you will lose the wit to follow 'ethereal finger-pointings', and you will forfeit the natural human right to transformation.

Again, the detached voice – a detached voice unafraid of declaring itself situated inside individual human experience – knows what it is like to 'glut thy sorrow on a morning rose,/Or on the rainbow of the salt sand-wave'. There is not necessarily any lack of respect for empirical evidence. Keats knows as well as any learned disciple of Isaac Newton (1642-1727) what salt crystals do to light. There is most definitely a sense of wonder, as exemplified by the 'wealth of globed peonies.' A peony can be, to Keats, a whole (other) world – and he can bring its whole other worldliness into being in the reader's imagination by spinning the suggestive 'globe' on a different – though unforced – axis of discourse. To the literal-minded, the double-exposure of microcosm and macrocosm can seem unhelpful. But Blake spoke a visionary language closely-related to Keats's when he saw a world in a grain of sand.

Keats sees transience everywhere, but looks past it to what it symbolises ('Ay, in the very temple of delight/Veil'd Melancholy has her Sovran shrine,/Though seen of none … ') just as the philosopher looks past the astronomer's stars and statistics to what they symbolise. Again, Blake knew, and said, as much:

> Joy and woe are woven fine,
> A clothing for the soul divine.
> Under every grief and pine
> Runs a joy with silken twine. (*Auguries of Innocence*)

A trophy is something to be won – a material object to be hoisted aloft in triumph in front of cheering spectators. At the conclusion of 'Ode on Melancholy', the reader is left with 'cloudy trophies hung' in the mind. In protecting the purity of the unspecific, the poet has left no metaphorical mantelpiece upon which these prizes would otherwise have been obliged to be displayed, sooner or later having their nimbus dissolved by the inevitable dust-layer of familiarity. Shelley used clouds as the very image of mutability ('We are as clouds that veil the midnight moon;/How restlessly they speed, and gleam, and quiver'); Hamlet saw in a cloud the shape of a camel one moment, a weasel the next moment, and a whale the next. Clouds have a poetic pedigree that goes as far back as Aristophanes. Poets' language can be cloudy, simultaneously concealing and revealing reality. In 'Ode to Autumn', the poet invokes the slanting rays of an autumnal sun which at once veils and venerates ('mists' *and* 'fruitfulness') what it shines upon: 'barred clouds bloom the soft-dying day'. Even the most impressive trophies of the material world will be changed as the light by which they are beheld changes – and, not least, as the beholder changes, as s/he is inextricably involved in the being of what s/he beholds. The trophies of the imagination gleam by what Thomas Traherne (1637-74) thought of as the 'Ministry of Inward Light'.

19

'Lamia'

Apollonius stands for intellect and reason; Lamia stands for emotion and sensation. Lamia can devour men. One thing that gives 'Lamia' (1819) its power is that Keats has never felt more divided: he knows that the grand truths arrived at by scientists such as Newton and philosophers such as William Godwin (1756-1836) can be used for the greater good of society. He also knows that poetry is not science or philosophy, and therefore the good of poetry is harder to identify – if it really exists at all, except in the (vain?) poet's imagination. (Arnold the school inspector and Carlyle the political philosopher – more than *mere* poets – would learn how to finger the stops of their trumpets.)

As John Whale has said, 'In giving the poem her name, Keats declares his interest in the nature of his Lamia.' (*Critical Issues: John Keats*, p.79) The following famous passage suggests that Keats's sympathies lie with Lamia:

> Do not all charms fly
> At the mere touch of cold philosophy?
> There was an awful rainbow once in heaven:
> We know her woof, her texture; she is given
> In the dull catalogue of common things.
> Philosophy will clip an Angel's wings,
> Conquer all mysteries by rule and line,
> Empty the haunted air, and gnomed mine –
> Unweave a rainbow, as it erewhile made
> The tender-person'd Lamia melt into a shade. (II, 229-38)

The beauty and acuity in Keats's poetry will, like Lamia, 'melt into … shade' if it is elucidated only by school inspectors or other professionals with the crude, insistent passion to hold their ground and register their disrespect for the 'bad' and the 'weak'. The 'progress' of place-hunting humanity can often look impressive (or imposing) on state-generated charts; but *is* the education available in the western world entirely blameless for the masses of uniformly uninteresting adults? To enumerate the amount of Angels' wings that have been clipped, and the weightless mental riches that have been confiscated, would be, of course, impossible. In such a climate, coffee has become proverbial because so many young people – finding little nourishment in the received opinion routinely dispensed at schools and universities – have been offered the practical advice to wake up and smell it.

At the time of writing 'Lamia', Keats (like Blake, Coleridge and Shelley) perceived 'progress' to be proliferating like cancer cells into the collective mind from the central theses of educationists. Three years earlier, on 28 December 1817, at the famous 'immortal dinner' given by Haydon, Keats had complained about Haydon's unfinished painting, 'Christ's Entry into Jerusalem'. Haydon had painted into the crowd the heads of Keats, Wordsworth, Hazlitt, Newton and Voltaire (1694-1778). Emboldened by a few glasses of wine, Charles Lamb wondered aloud why Haydon would include Newton in his painting, 'a Fellow who believed nothing unless it was as clear as the three sides of a triangle'. Keats responded in agreement by saying that Newton 'had destroyed all the poetry of the rainbow, by reducing it to a prism'. They drank 'Newton's health and confusion to mathematics'. There was much inspired talk on that 'evening worthy of the Elizabethan age', including much wit and humour, but Keats was already working through his thoughts in preparation for an important work.

Lamia's metamorphosis from a serpent into a woman displays again Keats's impressive rapport with Milton's *Paradise Lost*:

> Left to herself, the serpent now began
> To change; her elfin blood in madness ran,
> Her mouth foam'd, and the grass, therewith besprent,
> Wither'd at dew so sweet and virulent;
> Her eyes in torture fix'd, and anguish drear,
> Hot, glaz'd, and wide, with lid-lashes all sear,
> Flash'd phosphor and sharp sparks, without one cooling tear.
> The colours all inflam'd throughout her train,
> She writh'd about, convuls'd with scarlet pain:
> A deep volcanian yellow took the place
> Of all her milder mooned body's grace;
> And, as the lava ravishes the mead,

Spoilt all her silver mail, and golden brede;
Made gloom of all her frecklings, streaks and bars,
Eclips'd her crescents, and lick'd up her stars:
So that, in moments few, she was undrest
Of all her sapphires, greens, and amethyst,
And rubious-argent: of all these bereft,
Nothing but pain and ugliness were left.
Still shone her crown; that vanished, also she
Melted and disappear'd as suddenly … (I, 146-66).

Whale is insightful: 'There's a disturbing inversion at work here: in a story of a man-eating predatory lamia one might legitimately expect the narrative to begin with the putting on of a disguise of false beauty with which to lure and deceive the hapless male prey. Instead, Keats has his creature lose its dazzling beauty so as to become a woman.' (*Critical Issues: John Keats*, p.81) The tonal instability, over which the immature author of *Endymion* and 'Isabella' had significantly less control, is now fixedly and fluidly part of the mature poet's repertoire. Lamia is only *confoundingly* multi-faceted because that, for Keats, is the point:

She was a Gordian shape of dazzling hue,
Vermillion-spotted, golden, green, and blue;
Striped like a zebra, freckled like a pard,
Eyed like a peacock, and all crimson barr'd;
And full of silver moons, that, as she breathed,
Dissolv'd, or brighter shone, or interwreathed
Their lustres with the gloomier tapestries –
So rainbow-sided, touch'd with miseries,
She seem'd, at once, some penanced lady elf,
Some demon's mistress, or the demon's self.
Upon her crest she wore a wannish fire
Sprinkled with stars, like Ariadne's tiar:
Her head was serpent, but ah, bitter-sweet!
She had a woman's mouth … (I, 47-60).

The apparently unfixed subjects of Keats's poetry can find a different mode of definition against the backdrop of his letters:

… I do not think myself more in the right than other people and … nothing in the world is provable … I am sometimes so very sceptical as to think Poetry itself a mere Jack a lanthern to amuse whoever may chance to be struck with its brilliance – As Tradesmen say every thing is worth what it will fetch, so probably every mental pursuit takes its reality and worth from the ardour of the pursuer – being in itself a nothing – Ethereal thing may at least be thus real, divided under three heads – Things real – things semireal – and no things – Things real – such as existences of Sun Moon & Stars and passages of Shakspeare – Things semireal such as Love, the Clouds &c which require a greeting of the Spirit to make them wholly exist – and Nothings which are made Great and dignified by ardent pursuit … (*Letters*, I, pp.242-3).

In the light of this passage, from Keats's letter of March 1818 to Bailey, perhaps it would not be sensible or appropriate to inquire what 'Lamia' is 'of' or 'about', in the way, say, that one might interrogate Wordsworth's narrative poems such as 'The Mad Mother', 'The Idiot Boy', and 'We Are Seven', and find that they are 'of' and 'about' the thoughts and feelings of Britain's poorest and least articulate citizens.

Keats told his brother he was 'certain there is that sort of fire in it ['Lamia'] which must take hold of people in some way – give them either pleasant or unpleasant sensation. What they want is sensation of some sort' (*Letters*, II, p.189). Keats saw himself as a provider of this need: 'A Poet is the most unpoetical of any thing in existence; because he has no Identity – he is continually in for – and filling some other Body – The Sun, the Moon, the Sea and Men and Women who are creatures of impulse are poetical and have about them an unchangeable attribute – the poet has none; no identity … ' (*Letters*, I, p.387). But he knew that his 'Lamia' was – howsoever inspired, like the rest of his best poetry – not fiery in a way that would quickly cut through the hard, passionless clatter of contemporary thinking, and win him the recognition he deserved.

20

'La Belle Dame Sans Merci'

'La Belle Dame Sans Merci' means 'Beautiful Lady Without Pity.' For poets, death is a lady who must finally come for you. This poem is about death and the dying, and the dead. Keats wrote about what he saw in a dream. The poem is about him, and so deeply personal that he did not want to publish it. He is too young to die. He will not have achieved, in his mind, what he set out to do:

> And this is why I sojourn here
>   Alone and palely loitering,
> Though the sedge is wither'd from the lake,
>   And no birds sing. (XII)

The phrase 'Alone and palely loitering' is as haunting as Coleridge's 'Alone, alone all, all alone' – as if it has been echoing, all along, through the unsounded reaches of one's nervous system until a Keats, or a Coleridge, brought it into consciousness.

The spirit of the German love poet Tannhäuser (c.1200-c.1270) informs this magical, mysterious and painful ballad. The poem seems to be a – if not the – source of the Pre-Raphaelites such as Algernon Charles Swinburne (1837-1909) and the Symbolists such as Gustave Moreau (1826-98). In 1887, William Michael Rossetti (1829-1919) appreciated the potent charm of the poem: 'This is a poem of *impression*. The impression is immediate, final, and permanent; and words would be more than wasted upon pointing out to the reader that such and such are the details which have conduced to impress him … ' (*Keats: Narrative Poems*, p.65).

The reader may learn the poem by heart easily enough, and possess it, and be possessed by it, allowing the incantation to find its full psychic purchase in the combination of imagination, intellect and nervous energy that characterises a reader's receptivity to poetry. However, as is the case with Coleridge's 'Kubla Khan' (1797) and 'The Rime of the

Ancyent Mariner' (1798), whenever one tries to understand the poem, one discovers that one is trying to apply a formula to something that evades the formula. To ask what it 'means' is as misguided an approach as asking what a dream 'means' – or what a new planet that swims into one's ken means. It shape-shifts actively and echoically, and will not passively have its shape shifted into a final, defining passage of prose.

On one level, there appears to be a clash of discourses between the Belle Dame and the knight: 'She look'd at me as she did love,/And made sweet moan.' (VI) *Did* she love? What did the moan mean? (Does the presence of the adjective 'sweet' really do anything to answer the question?) If the reader is inclined to accept that the poem is about sex and death, s/he will understand that 'She' is coming – *le petit mort*. Does 'She' love him? (Does the presence of the word 'sure' really do anything to answer the question?) 'And sure in language strange she said –/"I love thee true." ' (VII) When did the dream begin? At what exact moment did the real turn into the unreal, reality into reverie? Where was the border? Where is the border?

The pressure of unanswered questions is like the presence of the dark – and death – that envelopes the figures in Rembrandt's (1606-69) 'Anatomy Lesson of Dr Tulp' (1632) or 'Night Watch' (1642). We are surrounded at all times by Mystery. We live in – and only in – Mystery. And we feel – or *will* feel – pain frequently: 'And I awoke, and found me here/On the cold hill side.' (XI) We do not know why we are here (to say nothing of the question of *if* we are here, or anywhere, or if the question why? has any validity).

When one experiences the desolation of being left by one's lover for ever, one is not actually left on a hill side; but one may recognise – having palely loitered on one's own version of it, perhaps – Keats's hill side. Shakespeare caught it earlier: Juliet was Romeo's 'Sun', and her extinction meant his extinction. Such a metaphor never – like a material reality – loses its lustre or shape over the centuries, or even millennia, but keeps all its value, and even retains and renews it. This is what Keats has in mind in the following letter:

> I will call the *world* a School instituted for the purpose of teaching little children to read – I will call the *human heart* the *horn Book* used in that School – and I will call the *Child able to read, the Soul* made from that *school* and its *hornbook*. Do you not see how necessary a World of Pains and troubles is to school an Intelligence and make it a soul? A Place where the heart must feel and suffer in a thousand diverse ways! (*Letters*, II, p.102)

Like Frank Osbaldistone in Scott's novel, *Rob Roy* (1817), many young people find themselves accountable to their parents – as, later on, they will find themselves accountable to the other funders of their activities. In the exacting realm of utility, mono-dimensional reading habits are instilled in people. So it is all the more remarkable that poems such as the 'Ode to a Nightingale', 'Ode to Autumn' or 'La Belle Dame Sans Merci' show the irreducibility of fine Romantic art to one 'meaning'. Keats's poetry is indicative of his (and the Romantic Movement's) resistance to an ethos unpropitious to all human beings but those who conceive themselves in terms of a mechanistic science. Keats has been in the grip of the muse, and living in a state of imaginative exaltation deriving in part from his visionary sense, and the rising towards the surface of unconscious themes. In 'La Belle Dame Sans Merci', he gives utterance to the unformulated content of the unconscious state of many individuals, a mélange of mortal anxiety and somnambulist eroticism. He felt 'more and more every day, as my imagination strengthens, that I do not live in this world alone but in a thousand worlds' (*Letters*, I, p.403). As Jung would put it in *The Undiscovered Self*, 'Such a condition cries out for order and synthesis.' Keats has answered the cries with some of the most beautiful and powerful poetry ever composed.

Select Reading

This book went to press just before the publication of Nicholas Roe's magnificent *John Keats: A New Life* and is poorer as a result.

John Keats: The Poetical Works, edited by H.W. Garrod (Oxford University Press, 1958)

The Letters of John Keats, 1814-1821, edited by H.E. Rollins (Harvard University Press, 1958)

Keats's Poetry and Prose, selected and edited by Jeffrey N. Cox (Norton, 2009)

Bate, Walter Jackson *John Keats* (Harvard University Press, 1963)

Butler, Marilyn *Romantics, Rebels & Reactionaries* (Oxford University Press, 1981)

Christiansen, Rupert *Romantic Affinities* (1994)

Ford, George H. *Keats and the Victorians: A Study of His Influence and Rise to Fame, 1821-1895* (Yale University Press, 1944, reprinted 1962)

Gittings, Robert *John Keats* (Penguin, 1967)

Goellnicht, Donald C. *The Poet-Physician: Keats and Medical Science* (University of Pittsburgh Press, 1984)

Hay, Daisy *Young Romantics: The Shelleys, Byron and Other Tangled Lives* (Bloomsbury, 2011)

Hazlitt, William *Spirit of the Age* (1825); ed. E.D. Mackerness (Northcote House, Plymouth, 1991)

Hill, John Spencer (ed.), *Keats: Narrative Poems* (Palgrave Macmillan, 1983)

Hunt, Leigh *Selected Writings*, edited by David Jesson-Dibley (Fyfield Books, 1990)

Jeffrey, Francis *On English Poets And Poetry* (not dated)

Matthews, G.M. (ed.), *Keats: The Critical Heritage* (Routledge, 1971)

Motion, Andrew *Keats* (Faber, 1997)

Patterson, Charles I. *The Daemonic in the Poetry of Keats* (University of Illinois Press, 1970)

Ricks, Christopher *Keats and Embarrasment* (Oxford University Press, 1974)

Roe, Nicholas *John Keats and the Culture of Dissent* (Oxford University Press, 1997)

The Poetical Works of Shelley, ed. Newell F. Ford (The Houghton Mifflin Company, Boston, 1974)

The Letters of Percy Bysshe Shelley, ed. Frederick L. Jones, 2 volumes (Oxford: Clarendon Press, 1964)

Ward, Aileen *John Keats: The Making of a Poet* (Viking Press, 1963)

Whale, John *Critical Issues: John Keats* (Palgrave Macmillan, 2005)

Index

GREENWICH EXCHANGE BOOKS

STUDENT GUIDE LITERARY SERIES

The Greenwich Exchange Student Guide Literary Series is a collection of essays on major or contemporary serious writers in English and selected European languages. The series is for the student, the teacher and the 'common reader' and is an ideal resource for libraries. The *Times Educational Supplement* praised these books, saying, "The style of [this series] has a pressure of meaning behind it. Readers should learn from that … If art is about selection, perception and taste, then this is it."

The series includes:
Antonin Artaud by Lee Jamieson (978-1-871551-98-3)
W.H. Auden by Stephen Wade (978-1-871551-36-5)
Jane Austen by Pat Levy (978-1-871551-89-1)
Honoré de Balzac by Wendy Mercer (978-1-871551-48-8)
Louis de Bernières by Rob Spence (978-1-906075-13-2)
William Blake by Peter Davies (978-1-871551-27-3)
The Brontës by Peter Davies (978-1-871551-24-2)
Robert Browning by John Lucas (978-1-871551-59-4)
Lord Byron by Andrew Keanie (978-1-871551-83-9)
Samuel Taylor Coleridge by Andrew Keanie (978-1-871551-64-8)
Joseph Conrad by Martin Seymour-Smith (978-1-871551-18-1)
William Cowper by Michael Thorn (978-1-871551-25-9)
Charles Dickens by Robert Giddings (987-1-871551-26-6)
Emily Dickinson by Marnie Pomeroy (978-1-871551-68-6)
John Donne by Sean Haldane (978-1-871551-23-5)
Elizabethan Love Poets by John Greening (978-1-906075-52-1)
Ford Madox Ford by Anthony Fowles (978-1-871551-63-1)
Sigmund Freud by Stephen Wilson (978-1-906075-30-9)
The Stagecraft of Brian Friel by David Grant (978-1-871551-74-7)
Robert Frost by Warren Hope (978-1-871551-70-9)
Patrick Hamilton by John Harding (978-1-871551-99-0)
Thomas Hardy by Sean Haldane (978-1-871551-33-4)
Seamus Heaney by Warren Hope (978-1-871551-37-2)

FOCUS ON SERIES

(ISBN prefix 978-1-906075 applies to all the following titles):

Jane Austen: *Mansfield Park* by Anthony Fowles (61-3)
James Baldwin: *Go Tell It on the Mountain* by Neil Root (44-6)
William Blake: *Songs of Innocence and Experience* by Matt Simpson (26-2)
Charlotte Brontë: *Jane Eyre* by Philip McCarthy (60-6)
Emily Brontë: *Wuthering Heights* by Matt Simpson (10-1)
Angela Carter: *The Bloody Chamber and Other Stories* by Angela Topping
  (25-5)
Truman Capote: *Breakfast at Tiffany's* by Neil Root (53-8)
The Poetry of John Clare by Angela Topping (48-4)
George Eliot: *Middlemarch* by John Axon (06-4)
T.S. Eliot: *The Waste Land* by Matt Simpson (09-5)
F. Scott Fitzgerald: *The Great Gatsby* by Peter Davies (29-3)
Michael Frayn: *Spies* by Angela Topping (08-8)
The Poetry of Robert Graves by Michael Cullup (60-9)
Thomas Hardy: *Poems of 1912–13* by John Greening (04-0)
Thomas Hardy: *Tess of the D'Urbervilles* by Philip McCarthy (45-3)
The Poetry of Tony Harrison by Sean Sheehan (15-6)
The Poetry of Ted Hughes by John Greening (05-7)
Aldous Huxley: *Brave New World* by Neil Root (41-5)
James Joyce: *A Portrait of the Artist as a Young Man* by Matt Simpson (07-1)
John Keats: *Isabella; or, the Pot of Basil, The Eve of St Agnes,*
  Lamia and *La Belle Dame sans Merci* by Andrew Keanie (27-9)
V.S. Naipaul: *A Bend in the River* by John Harding (74-3)
The Poetry of Mary Leapor by Stephen Van-Hagen (35-4)
Harold Pinter by Lee Jamieson (16-3)
Jean Rhys: *Wide Sargasso Sea* by Anthony Fowles (34-7)
The Poetry of Jonathan Swift by Stephen Van-Hagen (57-6)
Edward Thomas by John Greening (28-6)
Wordsworth and Coleridge: *Lyrical Ballads* (1798) by Andrew Keanie (20-0)

Other subjects covered by Greenwich Exchange books
Biography
Education
Philosophy